LOSING JAMES
A FATHER CRIES TOO

LOSING JAMES
A FATHER CRIES TOO

by

Michael Bollom

Bound Biographies

ISBN: 978-1-905178-38-4

Printed in Great Britain by the MPG Books Group,
Bodmin and King's Lynn

DEDICATION

This book is dedicated to

James

Love You

X

This book is for anyone who has suffered the loss of a child, in the hope that it gives some comfort and strength to continue life – and in the belief that we will all see our loved ones again one day.

We thought of you with love today,
But that is nothing new.
We thought about you yesterday,
And days before that too.
We think of you in silence,
We often speak your name.
Now all we have are memories,
And your picture in a frame.
Your memory is our keepsake,
With which we'll never part;
God has you in his keeping,
But we have you in our hearts.

Author unknown

FOREWORD

Children bring us so much pleasure as they grow up and become young adults. Sadly, I never met James Bollom, who was a young man who embraced life and lived it to the full. However, I have been privileged to meet James' dad, Michael. Through my conversations with Michael, and reading this book, I feel that I have come to know this popular young man whose big smile and friendly personality enabled him to shine in company of all ages. James was someone with many interests, a zest for life and for new experiences. As a parent myself, I can appreciate how special the close relationship was that James experienced with his dad. As such, I can empathise with the agonies of loss experienced by Michael when James was killed outright at the age of 16. His shock is palpable throughout a book which conveys to the reader the impact of James' short life on those around him, whilst somehow managing to rise above the sadness involved around James' death to become a celebration of his life and a comfort and hope to anyone who has lost a beloved child.

It is difficult to find any written help that acknowledges the impact of a child's death on their father who is left behind. Fathers grieve too. This book offers an insight through the numbing grief that suddenly overwhelms and threatens to consume all who loved a child. Michael eloquently leads the reader through the stages of grief he experienced, together with the support he received and continues to receive from others who loved James. Michael also gradually discovered help from unexpected sources, finding comfort and an unequivocal conviction that life goes on after death, in some form, within the spiritual realm.

I recommend this uplifting account of a father's love to anyone who has a child in their lives. We need to love completely and unreservedly in order to make each day count.

Sue Ginman 2009

CONTENTS

My World Changes

"Pull over! Pull over!" was all I could hear coming from the back seat as I was shouting into the phone. My mind was a whirl – I was hearing all these different voices but not really understanding exactly what each one was saying. All I could understand was, "He's dead! He's dead!" coming from the voice of my ex-wife Samantha on the other end of the line.

I was on the outside carriageway of the A2 in Kent returning from an overnight stay in London. I am not even sure that I looked in my mirror but my instinct was to swerve the car onto the hard shoulder. Louise was in the back with Nicki. I was driving with Rob in the front. I pulled up – don't even remember getting out of the car as something kicks in and takes control of you when you hear something like that.

Even though I heard what Samantha was telling me, my brain did not soak it in. It just kind of hung around in my head – maybe I did not want to absorb or even believe what she was saying.

I jumped out of the car and paced up and down the hard shoulder shouting into the phone. The others got out of the car and just stood and watched, mesmerised by what was going on and by what I was saying. I had been trying for hours to get hold of James on his mobile and I knew something was not right.

Samantha was still shouting, "He's dead! He's dead!" Of course there was no way I was going to believe her – she obviously had got it totally wrong. She said the police were there with her and I asked for the phone to be handed over so I could make some sense of why she was saying this. A police family liaison officer came on – I didn't even take any notice of his name at the time – I just wanted answers as to why Samantha was saying James was dead...He apologised for me finding out in this way but went on to tell me that James had been involved in an 'RTA', or road traffic accident to you and me.

We can deal with that – we will get him the best medical care possible and after a while he will be fine. These things happen all the time – we've all had near misses. But at the back of my mind I knew what he was really trying to tell me – I just did not want to believe it. This doesn't happen to someone like me – to a family like mine – what have we ever done to deserve this?

I kept asking and asking: Where was he? Was he alright? What hospital was he in? And the police officer kept reiterating that I had not understood what he was saying. He explained that he had not wished for me to find out in this way but it was taken out of his hands. I glanced towards Lou, Rob and Nic who all had tears rolling down their faces – they couldn't bear to see me in such a state but never did they expect this, either. Louise asked how he was. "He's dead," I said. Everyone cried uncontrollably on the roadside.

James was in an RTA and had been killed instantly.

My world as I knew it ended at 4.15pm on Sunday 4th December 2005.

JAMES

James was born on 9th January 1989 and christened James Joseph Bollom – Joseph after his grandad, my dad, as he was the first grandchild. Samantha and I were overjoyed. Being a firstborn and a first grandchild, James was someone very, very special, a child to be proud of.

We lived near to my parents in Arkley, Hertfordshire. I worked in the family leisure business alongside my father and we were a very close family. My sisters all lived nearby and James never wanted for anything. He was thoroughly spoilt by us and by his grandparents and I look back now with ease that I gave him everything he needed. If I had continually said no to everything he asked for, I truly believe it would have haunted me 17 years later.

Throughout James' early life, times were shared with his grandfather who took him out most weekends, whether it was just round to his own house or to local parks and zoos. James always held a special place in my father's heart – maybe it was because he was the first grandson, or perhaps it was James' personality that kept his grandad hooked into James' life right up until the day he died.

I was very proud and very protective of James and played as equally an active role as Samantha in bringing James up: having Dad days with just him and me, and getting him interested in gadgets that were available to buy. My day was a Sunday and we would get up and drive somewhere, just the two of us whilst his mum had a break and prepared lunch. We would sometimes go to Regents Park where he liked the swings and he always got excited about feeding the ducks.

His mother always played the role of making sure activities were done after school.

James made many friends along the way from activities like tennis and swimming lessons, to name a couple. James was never a boy who was interested in football; still, neither was I. Friends had season tickets to Tottenham so I thought it would be a good idea to buy two for James and me. After a few matches, James being James got bored – a couple of matches after that, so did I. I was the most popular person in White Hart Lane trying to give the tickets away!

James attended Goodwyn School in Mill Hill, North London, to start with and then moved on to Radlett Preparatory School in Hertfordshire. Both schools were close by and James absolutely loved Radlett Prep. He was not the best of pupils. I knew he was never going to cure cancer or stop global warming but he was always well liked, acting up as the class clown as he had no attention span whatsoever, but all the teachers loved him, commenting on what a great smile he had.

James' academic marks were considered average but we always knew he would make his way in the world as he had the gift of the gab. He participated in most activities and was always the first to put his hand up when assistance was required for anything at school – mainly to get out of homework or class, but nonetheless he was always willing and helpful.

We had a close-knit group of friends around us in Arkley, who we would go away on holidays with or meet up with of a weekend; James would thrive on the company and could easily hold his own with adult conversation from a very young age.

We were lucky enough to have a pool in the garden and James learned to swim early in life. On holidays, all he would do was go in the water whether it was the sea or the pool. My parents had a holiday home in Fort Lauderdale, Florida, which was looked after by an elderly neighbour when we were not there. Our neighbour in Florida, Estelle, idolised James and called him 'Sir James', much to his annoyance and embarrassment as he grew older. She would beg to take him out for an evening whilst we were there. Once I remember she took him to the cinema. We met them afterwards. When Estelle came out, she had little bits of rolled-up paper all over her hair. Being grateful that she had made the effort to take James out for the evening, I never said anything as I thought she must have known. I questioned James on it later in the evening… he advised that after watching 'Iron Giant' for 20 minutes he had got so bored he decided to chew the wrapper from his straw and then propel rolled-up pieces of it into Estelle's bouffant hairstyle. That was James' sense of humour to a tee. The poor woman had to endure an hour of James firing paper at her and she didn't even realise.

Many years later, when on a day trip with my father, James, and Louise's dad, Neil, we were driving along and Neil looked flushed even though it was a fairly cool day outside. He was in the front seat next to me fidgeting and looking rather uncomfortable as if he was unwell. I asked him if he was OK. "No, not really," was his reply, "My arse feels as if it's on fire." When I looked down, I noticed the heated seat had been on the whole trip. I glanced in the mirror and could see James smirking on the back seat. Many years later this incident was to repeat itself, but more about that later. James was a prankster and loved to play jokes at everyone's expense. He was known for his sense of humour. Most young boys considered 'Transformers' or 'Power Rangers' to be their favourite TV programmes. James listed 'Candid Camera' and 'Beadle's About' amongst his.

James had a smile though that meant that, whatever he did, you could not be angry with him. To earn extra pocket money he would ask if he could clean the cars. One weekend I let him do the whole car which had brilliant white wall tyres on it. I explained that the white wall tyres had to be cleaned with Brillo pads to make them pure white. I kept an eye on James as he cleaned the bodywork, leathered it off and I thought, Great, he knows what he's doing. Luckily I glanced out just as he was finishing his first tyre. Instead of cleaning the white wall on the actual tyre itself with Brillo pads, James had decided to scrub the entire alloy wheel. Funnily enough, it did not produce a shine so he scrubbed harder and harder until the entire wheel was scratched to pieces. However, once he had flashed his smile I could not be angry with him for long and realised it was my own fault for not making myself clear. He still earned his pocket money but got out of cleaning the car for a long while thereafter.

When James was about seven, I took him skiing with friends and their sons – an all-male trip. Unbeknown to me, Samantha had obviously not been happy with her life or our marriage. She had everything a wife could wish for: a lovely five-bed home with a housekeeper, a top-of-the-range convertible, foreign holidays at least three times a year but …

It was when we came back from a great trip that I noticed things were not quite the same. I knew something was up but I was not going to believe it. I ignored the situation for weeks and weeks until one day she confessed to having an affair. Now, in this situation, when you have much love for your wife and fully embrace your role as the 'keeper', so to speak, of your family, you are not going to let your marriage fail. Forgiveness was my priority – but I learned, over many months of trying, that when the love has gone it will never return and I knew there was nothing I could do to kick-start our relationship. I now know that was how Samantha felt too.

This, as is usually the case, turned into a very messy divorce. I tried to keep James sheltered from this, but when there are rows going on and an atmosphere in the house, he was obviously bound to notice something was not right. After a while James and Samantha moved out of the family home. I wanted James to remain with me but I knew, had it gone to court, this would never have been granted. However, he came to stay with me nearly every night whilst Samantha settled into her new life.

As time passed, eventually the divorce was resolved in court with a conclusion meaning that we could both move on whilst ensuring James was, and would remain throughout his life, our Number One priority.

As far as James was concerned, there were no access restrictions and all was agreed without court intervention, which was a blessing as this made the effect on James minimal; he knew he could come and go as he pleased. I think, after realising he would have two lots of birthday and Christmas presents, it eased his mind somewhat!

The divorce left us living in different areas. With the sale of the family home, Samantha and James moved to a house in Brickett Wood near Radlett, Herts, about ten minutes from the original family home. This meant that James would remain in the same location as his friends and at the same school. Samantha remained with the partner she had left me for.

After some months, I too met a new partner, Louise, and I decided to change my roots and move down to Kent. Louise lived and worked in Kent and I thought the upheaval would be less if I moved – had it not worked out for whatever reason, I could simply move back. I made sure that this did not affect James and felt that it would be good for him meeting new friends. I also knew that whatever time I spent with James would be pure quality time.

James was very comfortable around Louise as she made him feel special. He was, and he had accepted the fact that Louise and I were going to live together in the new home. We made James' bedroom a replica of his old bedroom in Radlett, even down to the curtain fabric, and he immediately felt at home. The cul-de-sac we lived in was full of children and all he ever wanted to do was go out and play. Louise's friends locally had children so we would arrange picnics, games in the park, barbeques – the normal family things. James was in his element, and he would stay with us every weekend. I would collect him from school on a Friday and take him to school on Monday. He never wanted to leave as he was so comfortable in Kent. On Wednesdays I would have him at my mum and dad's house as it gave them a chance to see him during the week.

After a couple of years of me living in Kent, James passed his exams and left Radlett Prep, moving to St Columbus School in St Albans. I felt he was unhappy there as he missed his friends from Radlett Prep and only one other boy had chosen this new school. He also found the school very strict compared to the junior school he had moved from, and every Monday I found it harder and harder to get him up for school at 5.30 am to drive up to London. Not being an academic, the school was too much for James – he seemed to thrive in smaller, family-run schools, the sort of environment which his other two schools had been.

James made many friends and liked it a lot in Kent, so much so that he persuaded his mum to rethink where they lived and move down as well. Sam was originally from Chatham in Kent anyway, so this was not going to be an impossibility, especially when she eventually split from her new partner.

I immediately went looking in the West Malling area which was close to me but not too close. This way, Samantha could start a new life without us being on one another's doorstep. Luckily there were houses being built in the area which were suitable. In fact, the houses seemed far bigger and better value than in London and I verbally reserved a house I thought she would like. She loved it and within a week we had the other house on the market and made an offer on the West Malling house.

Bingo! It all happened together. Everyone pleased. Samantha was moving back to her roots, James would be near to me and could come and stay any time now, and schooling was to be arranged at Sackville School, Hildenborough, which I felt resembled his old junior school in Radlett – a lovely family environment in a school which was quite small – an atmosphere that James loved.

Finally, I felt that having James back close to me and not having to worry about his mum was a good move. James was 13 at this time. We were now all living in Kent enjoying the countryside. Bearsted to West Malling was 15 minutes away, three junctions down the M20, so no trouble in seeing James as and when I wished.

The same arrangements were to be put in place: Every Wednesday I would collect James from Sackville School and return him on Thursday, but now that he was close by, weekends became hit-and-miss as friends now started to take precedence. I always insisted he stayed at some point over the weekend as I missed him so much – however, James being a teenager, his mates were his life. This was not too much of a problem as I spoke with James at least once every day on his mobile phone.

The mobile was James' lifeline. James could easily have won a Vodaphone award for highest bills had there been one available. To say James loved mobile phones would be a dramatic understatement. I bought him his first phone at the age of ten – this may seem young but at the time it was the only way of speaking with him as it was right in the middle of our divorce. It was a 'pay as you go' – and 'go' James certainly did. To start with £10.00 every two weeks was ample as none of his friends had a phone. However, within a year, the top-up had crept up to £50 a week! My father then had the bright idea of getting James put onto a contract which he offered to pay. I reiterated that James liked to talk, but I don't think my father quite grasped the amount of time James liked to talk to his friends. Due to the amount of numbers on our contract, it was possible to obtain a very competitive tariff for James, or so we thought.

James used to keep in touch with his grandparents most days with his grandad calling many times during the week. He missed not living so close but saw James when we went up to Hertfordshire for Sunday lunch and vice versa. During these times James would hint about new phones. James was constantly on the net, always interested in the new Nokia phone – knowing he was now on contract, he realised you could get upgraded phones all the time. Of course, you had to pay for them, but he managed to persuade his grandad that it was a great investment as he could sell the old one on eBay as he was bound to make a profit! By this time all of his friends had mobile phones also.

James would change his phone regularly. He would use the upgrade of one of our sales rep's phones to get the phone he wanted, so some poor sod had to suffer an old mobile phone for the duration of working for us in order for James to have the latest technology! He was always the first to get the latest phone. When his friends asked what the phone was like, he would tell them it was rubbish as he did not want them to have the same!

Month after month a letter arrived from my dad addressed to James saying that he was spending too much on the phone bill – month after month James would convince him that he would cut back, and this became a regular cycle. We knew there was no way my dad was ever going to take the phone away from him, and of course so did James. Eventually, when the bills got so high, Dad called Vodaphone into the office – they were the best to advise what tariff James should go on. Oh no, there was no tariff that was equipped for the amount of calls James was making. In the end it was agreed that all inter-company mobile numbers would be free – great, but James only used to call Dad and me. Strangely enough, everyone at the local pub did not work for us, but you would never guess by the amount of times someone would call James and I'd hear him say, "I'll call you back to save your bill." Unfortunately, James never found that tree that grows money in the garden, but he obviously thought my father's was flourishing!

Apart from his mobile phone, James' other interest was mostly music, and oh how he loved his music! We saw a magazine article one year showing David Beckham wearing an iPod – none of us knew what it was as you could not get them in England at the time. Louise searched on the net and managed to buy one from America. James opened it and did not have a clue what it was – three days later it was full of songs. His iPod had over 3,000 songs on as well as photos and videos. He was obsessed with music and was always downloading. I sometimes thought that when he suddenly came home, it maybe wasn't always to see me but to download some new tracks he had heard that week as his iTunes store was on our computer at home. Still, I didn't mind.

Computing was always a heavy interest and when James was going into his final year he chose this subject. He was always showing me what to do and putting things right that I would do when he was not here. He seemed to pick up computing like a duck to water! Like anyone his age, he became addicted to MSN. We often thought how

10

studious he was as he spent all evening on the computer 'doing his homework'. Little did we know that he was chatting to every man and his dog!

James was very much a lover of fishing. He would drag his mum out to the fishing sites and sometimes persuade her to camp out all night – not her sort of thing but she did it for James. He took part in the fishing cup at school; however, unbeknown to us until months later, the winner was pre-selected each year according to who the fishing gang felt was the main man at the time! His fishing took James to France every year with the school – he would come home knackered as I think sleep had been the last thing on their minds! It was great to see James with a passion for fishing and each week he insisted that he needed a new gadget – Fox tent, Fox chair – everything had to be Fox (a top fishing brand that every fisherman wanted).

James and the one that did not get away

A typical teenager, James was always looking at ways to make money. He was not too keen on the 'working week' ethos so decided the easiest way was to send a video into 'You've been framed'. How hard could it be? James wrote out a list of embarrassing situations that he could film – all directed by himself, with us as the bemused victims ready to fall off a chair, get hit by a flying object or whatever situation he came up with that he thought was original and would get him a quick £250.00 – of course none were ever sent in as we managed to persuade him that ITV executives were not that stupid and that it would take a lot more than 'camera – action' from James Spielberg to get the money out of them!

Being in the leisure business myself, we were always visiting amusement parks as James loved the roller-coasters. Once a year we would go to the States and fly off to the latest park to 'test' the rides. He loved Disney, as any other child his age would, but as he grew older his holiday priorities changed. The apartment in Florida had strict rules and they became so ridiculous for a boy of James' age so we started to look elsewhere for our holidays.

We then made the mistake of taking James to Vegas. He loved it from the minute he walked off the plane. James was mesmerised by the hotels, the parks, the video games, the restaurants – you name it, he loved it. We stayed in the Bellagio Hotel which he came to love and would come to know like the back of his hand. Our friend worked at the Bellagio and would take James 'underground' to see the village for staff under the hotel. James was in total awe of the place. We would sit by the pool and watch him go off and make friends; he would come back with a gaggle of kids all in awe of him as he was the tallest and most street-wise.

Our friends Brian and Judy have lived in Vegas for many years and they adored James. He would fish in the lake by their house and befriended their grandchildren. He loved the fountains at the Bellagio, which sometimes played to music. In fact, the first time we stepped out of the cab on arriving at the Bellagio, I remember the track by Andrea Boccelli and Sarah Brightman playing 'Time to Say Goodbye' …little did I know at the time how significant this song was to become. The Bellagio had an arcade for kids, as they were too young to enter the casino. James made it his mission to win the biggest toy there. With hindsight, it would have been cheaper for me to buy the bloody toy outright!

Holidays were more moderate with his mum but that was how James liked it. They would go to places such as Corfu and do things they enjoyed together. Upon moving to West Malling, Sam met a new man, Mark, and they moved in together. I liked Mark as he was good for James in the same way Louise was, and most importantly he had respect for me as James' father, which I admired. Mark would say that if there was a problem with James and his mum and James was out of order, he would tell me and I was to deal with it. Mark never tried to act as James' dad – he was more a father-figure.

James often talked about what he wanted to do with his life. My father had a printing business that he secretly wished James would take over when he was old enough. James went there every school holiday to earn extra money. He would sweep the floor from one side of the factory to the other. Unbeknown to him, my dad was watching him on the CCTV when it came to filling up the vending machine. James would put one chocolate bar in the machine and one in his pocket. Dad swears that by the time the holiday was over, the profits of the company were down as James had polished off nearly every bar in the machine! Although James enjoyed the holiday work, printing was not something that interested him.

I had hoped James would work with me in my new business venture, which involved boats amongst other things. We had bought ourselves a boat in Kent and James loved it. Each weekend a different friend would come down and go out on the boat with us.

During the summer holidays we were asked to clean and prepare a new boat from Fairline Boats in Ipswich before it left for their customer overseas. James was really pleased to be involved. I thought we had now found his interest and we should build up this part of the company for his future. The product was called 'A Glaze' and we had the licence to sell the Marine version all over the world.

We took a small stand at the London Boat Show in January 2005 which James helped us with. We gave him the job of giving out leaflets to anyone he could. After Day Three the security stopped him and said he could not do the leaflet drops any more as it was not fair on the other exhibitors. James had covered nearly the whole of Excel! He was enjoying the challenge. A top boat manufacturer had asked us to prepare all of their stand boats at the show. We were now on our way, as they had agreed that this product was to be promoted by them on all new boats. I thought this was great as it provided a foundation to work on and was going to be ready for when James started full-time.

When we purchased a new factory in Sittingbourne James became very excited. He was assisting me with some floor painting in the factory and could see on the plans the desk area and phone number for himself. He was ready – James' own desk, with his own direct-dial phone number. This was immediately tapped into his mobile phone to text all his mates. James would come into the office every Wednesday once he finished school and started college – however, his phone line was always busy with mates rather than sales calls.

James also toyed with the idea of joining the army – mainly as they had open-top Cherokees and Land Rovers – until Louise and I pointed out that the Land Rovers would not necessarily have heated seats, air conditioning or blacked-out windows, and he wouldn't always get a roast on a Sunday!

After a number of years of living in Kent with Louise, I decided to ask her to marry me. James, of course, was consulted, but as he got on very well with Louise his blessing was overwhelming. I asked him if he would be my best man. He was very worried at such a task so it was agreed that he would be joint best man with my best mate John. James was 14.

The wedding day started in the usual way with family arriving at the home and James in his morning suit. He looked so handsome and I was very proud. James conducted himself so well and spoke to everyone and was not at all worried about the speech as he was not doing it. John had asked James to stand by his side and be the attractive one and he would be doing the talking. James stood there blushing during John's speech, as he was very complimentary about James, especially his looks and charm.

My wedding day with James as best man

The day went so well but at the end when we were to leave for the hotel I became very emotional. I do not know why, but maybe I was finally moving on now that James was settled in Kent. I was so proud of James that day as who knows what was going through his mind with his dad re-marrying. All I know is that James was happy for me and knew that he was special as he now had two families.

James and his grandad

James started to talk about driving, which became more important to him than what he wanted to do with his life. He started off wanting a Hummer, then it went to a Cherokee jeep – the open-top variety. It ranged from Range Rovers to sports cars, until James finally realised that he was going to have to get a car below the Group 4 insurance category! I had agreed with James that if he was never to ask for a motorbike I would buy him a car at the age of 17. Time to spoil him rotten, I know, but that is what I had agreed to do and it worked. Not that I have anything against motorbikes – I just feel that they would have been dangerous for James.

One Saturday morning we went hunting for cars. James had set his mind on a VW Golf and we ordered a brand-new one in black. His grandad bought him a roof spoiler to go on it, so for a first car he was not doing too badly. James was just so excited about the car: it went from black, then blue, then grey, then a call to Grandad, then his mum, then back to blue, his favourite colour, then finally back to black. Alloy wheels were also a big discussion. We were there for at least an hour filling in the order form. He drove the sales guy mad!

Done. We walked out of the showroom with James' face beaming like a Cheshire cat. Delivery was planned for January, which would be in time for him to start his driving on the ninth, his 17th birthday.

Little did James know that a number plate JB 55 JJB had been bought in July. I think I was more excited than he was. I sometimes think that the giving person can be just as excited knowing how much pleasure a gift will give someone, especially if they are not expecting it.

I went back to the car dealership to arrange a Christmas delivery and also confirm the number plate to go on the car. It was all arranged to be delivered on Christmas Eve on trade plates, not being able to leave the garage till January 1st as that was the car's first registration day. That was fine: James would not have allowed anyone to have driven it anyway. We were all set.

James still thought he was going to get the car delivered in January so we planned to get him all the usual cleaning products, ask him to put them in the garage and hey presto! there would be his new car and number plates waiting for him. Brilliant plan. What could possibly go wrong?

James had left Sackville to attend Kent College and study Business Studies, as well as other things. During that same month my best friend Paul, who owns a Land Rover dealership in North London, leant me a supercharged Range Rover for the weekend to see if I liked it. I remember arriving in it at his college to collect James on a Friday afternoon. He was so excited. "WOW! WOW! Hang on Dad. Let me call my friends over." This car had only just come out and James had begged me to get one. It had everything on it. It was black with cream leather upholstery, DVD player and screens in the back. This car had every conceivable extra you could wish for and it was fast, very fast – supercharged. It was also very thirsty as well as expensive. "Oh come on Dad, you have to get one of these." Everything with James was a must: "You need one of these, Dad."

A heated discussion continued for several days and weeks after the car was returned back as a demonstrator. I thanked Paul for the loan. This was probably causing me more trouble than it was worth but James never let it drop. Every time we'd go out in what was now considered by James to be an outdated car, he would comment, "If only you had the supercharged…" James had a very childlike view of money; maybe this was the way I had made it for him, but he really thought I had a bottomless pit and should just go out and get the new car. Insurance costs, etc. meant nothing to James, and in a funny way it was a lovely way for him to be.

Thankfully, after some time the discussions dwindled as James was now looking forward to driving his own car.

IN THE BLINK OF AN EYE

For the first time in years, Louise and I went away for a weekend in London with friends Rob and Nic. Our day started with breakfast in the Dorchester Hotel. Very plush, we thought, but nice to treat ourselves once in a while. I had spoken with James the night before when he called as usual and wanted some info from Louise on an eBay question. The call was short and sweet: little did I know that it was the last time I would ever speak to him. We always finished our conversations by saying "Love you", before replacing the handset.

The following day we decided to have lunch in the main dining room before setting off back home. James was due to be collected by me in the afternoon as he was staying with us, so in the morning I called him as usual but the phone was not switched on. Strange, I thought, but never mind – after a Saturday night he was probably having a lie-in! I continued trying till lunchtime. Now the phone was ringing and ringing but no answer. I then called his other home. No answer and so I decided to call Samantha's mobile. Again, no answer. I felt uneasy not being able to make contact with anyone, but I thought there was probably some silly explanation.

We were all ready to leave and, to be honest, I couldn't get out of the door quick enough as my stomach was reeling and I was feeling uncomfortable. I tried once more on James' phone but it was just ringing and ringing. Our friend Ann, who comes and helps out with housework during the week, called my mobile to say the police had called her, looking for us. She had asked them what was wrong and they assured her there was nothing to worry about. We set off on our journey home and I asked Louise to call Ann back, just to check on what the police had actually said. Ann then gave us a number for the police and Louise called them. She spoke with a WPC who asked when we would be home and again assured her there was nothing to worry about. Louise and Nic were in the back of the car convinced that something was not right but, to be honest, they thought that maybe James had been playing pranks and had got into trouble. Never in a million years did it occur to us that something serious had happened.

I then tried James' phone again – still no answer. I was now beginning to panic and felt that things were very wrong. I had never gone this long without being able to get hold of him. Sometimes at his home James would get a bad signal, but this signal always came back. He would surely see my missed call and phone me back immediately, whatever he was doing.

We had now just gone through the Blackwell Tunnel and onto the A2. My phone rang and I saw the West Malling home number come up – relief at last, or so I thought. Samantha was screaming down the phone sobbing with the words, "James is dead." Although I had been unable to reach him on his mobile for hours, I never expected to hear these words. The way Sam spoke, I knew deep down her words were true but I just couldn't bring myself to believe it. I was crying into the phone, asking her what she meant. Why was she saying these things? Where was he? Samantha, of course, was beside herself – she would never have told me in this way otherwise.

A police officer came on the line. He had tried to contact me at my address as James' provisional licence had my address in Bearsted and he did not want me to be told in this way. Totally shell-shocked, I asked what had happened. The police officer said that James was a passenger in a car which had swerved onto the other side of the carriageway on the approach into Wateringbury, Kent. They were hit by an oncoming car as a result of which James suffered fatal injuries. I asked how badly hurt he was as your mind misses words when it is in a panic. He repeated that it was fatal. To be honest, I still did not understand or did not want to comprehend what he was telling me. I did not want to believe him, so I repeated my question with some firmness realising that everyone else was eager to know what had happened. "He is dead…" Maybe if I had been face to face with the officer I would have realised a lot sooner as his face would have said it all.

It is amazing how 'calm' you can be when you hear things like that. I think it is shock as no-one expects to get a phone call to say their son is dead – not in this way, whatever their age. Everything came together – the calls that James was not accepting, his phone being switched off, his mum's mobile not answering. All of it now made sense. It was as if my mind was like a combination on a safe. All of a sudden, everything just clicked into place and opened up my brain to realise what he was telling me. Looking back now, I realise that shock takes over and deep down you truly don't accept what is being told to you. It is like a bad dream and you hope you will awaken to find everything is back to normal.

I asked where James was now and the Family Liaison Officer, who I shall refer to throughout as Graham, said he was at Maidstone Hospital. He asked me to meet him there and he would talk to me more then. My near-perfect weekend had turned into a living nightmare. Was I being punished for having a good time? I now had to face reality. I would have to identify my 16-year-old son's body.

I did not cry as I spoke to the police officer as I don't think my body wanted to accept what was going on. It was totally surreal: something you see happening in a film – a horror film. Louise was asking me how he was and what had happened, as they had obviously heard bits of my conversation. "He's dead," was all I could say as if I was on autopilot. "He's been in a car accident and he's dead. I have to go to the hospital to identify him."

"Who was driving?" was Louise's first question. When I told her, she knew the boy was going too fast but that was put to the back of our minds. James was our first thought, as he had been throughout his entire life. Why should his death be any different?

We all stood, shell-shocked on the kerbside, an abrupt end to our weekend. The colour just drained from our faces. It was as if time had stood still for an hour. One minute we were laughing and joking, the next I was trying to absorb the fact that James was dead and I was never to speak with him ever again.

We got back in the car and Robert drove us to the hospital. The girls were in the back sobbing, with me in the front in a different world, not quite believing that my baby had been taken from me. Many questions were going through my head at a rate of a thousand thoughts a second, like Why? What? How?

I knew I had to call my father to tell him, as he would want to come straight down and be with me. Looking back, it was not a call I ever wanted to make, telling him this over the phone in the same way I found out, but I really did not know what I was doing. I explained the bad news that James had been killed in a car accident and that I wanted him to come down. He hung up and within a couple of minutes called back to tell me that my sister's husband, who was also called James, had been killed in a car accident. "No, Dad, not that James, *your* James," I said. With that he dropped the phone and I could hear the groaning and crying – my father's shock at the realisation that his beloved grandson was dead.

We proceeded to Maidstone Hospital with not a word said in the car. Everyone was in total shock, not knowing what to say as no-one had ever been in this situation before. We pulled up some 40 minutes later. I got out and Robert stayed with me. At first I did not want anyone there, not even Louise. Maybe that was my way of not accepting it was true. Who knows? The girls went home as family were to arrive very shortly. My sisters were coming down and Dad's friend, Les, was driving him and my mum down. John, my best man at our wedding, was also on his way down.

I had begged Sam to come to the hospital with me. I felt she needed too. If it was true and James really had been killed, then this would be our final goodbye whilst he was warm. We could hold him and tell him we loved him, kiss his warm skin and let him be at peace. She just couldn't do it. She knew it was James, as I did deep down, but by seeing him would be admitting to herself that he had gone.

The Family Liaison Officer, Graham, arrived in the police car and took me to one side. He said that I needed to identify James and that it might not be very pleasant as he was not aware of the extent of the injuries. I was placed in a small waiting room and offered the usual tea whilst he made his enquiries as to where James was. He eventually came back to say that the injuries from a viewing point of view were not as bad as he had thought and that anything too bad was now covered with a bandage. He asked me if I was ready. Of course I said yes, but in reality nothing prepares you for seeing your child lying motionless in a hospital room. In one way, I wanted to see him so much to talk to him in the hope that he could hear me, but in another way seeing him would confirm that it was James and that he really had gone.

We walked for what seemed forever through corridor after corridor. I was asking questions on why and how the car came to be across the other side of the road in the path of an oncoming car. It was too early to say but it appeared that the driver was travelling at speed and possibly hit a kerb or lost it on the corner. The driver did not have any life-threatening injuries, and little did I know, at that time, during that walk I had walked passed him and his parents. At the time I was in total oblivion and was blinkered as I just wanted to get the viewing over and done with.

We arrived at a room with a window. The curtains were drawn and I knew that we had arrived. Graham let me take my time to compose myself and enter the room to identify James. As I opened the door there was James lying in a bed with a bandage across the left side of his face, like Pudsey bear from Children in Need. I kissed him and cuddled him hoping it was a mistake. He was still warm and looked so peaceful, sound asleep, never to wake. I sobbed as I let my emotions finally take over.

There was I and my baby whom I had brought into the world, who had had such a future taken away from him in such a horrifying way, a way that could have been avoided. I loved him so much and the thought of him lying dead before me was unthinkable. You just never expect it. Why could I not have been there with him when he died to tell him I loved him so much? What if he had suffered? What if he hadn't died straightaway and had lain all alone in the car in pain? The thoughts were unbearable. Why did this have to happen to such a beautiful boy with a wonderful smile, big mischievous eyes and a loving manner? What had James ever done to deserve this?

I stayed for a short while but knew that I should now be with family and that I should also go and see Samantha. She needed me. I knew she was not the strongest person so this could have pushed her over the edge. We had just lost our only child whom we had both loved and doted on every day of his life. What was she going to do now?

Robert said his goodbyes and got a lift back home to Louise and Nic. Graham drove me to James' other home in West Malling.

The journey from Maidstone Hospital was a little fragile. I sat there on autopilot not really knowing what to say. My mind just kept going over and over the fact that James had been killed in a car accident at such a young age with his whole life ahead of him. I had only just met Graham, and not in the best of circumstances – what was I to say to him? Graham had asked me if I wanted to see where the accident had occurred. I declined at this time, knowing I had that experience to come later. I just didn't feel up to it. What if the scene was bad? I would not be able to forget about it and it would play on my mind that James might have suffered.

We drove straight to Samantha's house. Samantha and Mark were there with their friends, who had all come to pay their respects. It was strange going into a house with so many people I did not know, at a time when I really wanted around me only those that I knew. I did not want to engage in small talk, not today. It was also a difficult time as, apart from anything else, it would be the first time in many years that Samantha had been in my arms. We had just lost the only thing we had both cherished in the world, our beautiful boy. Whatever had gone on in the past did not matter that evening as nothing could change the sequence of events today.

We sat in James' bedroom crying together, sobbing uncontrollably. I smelt his tee shirt that was lying on his bed. The sense of his smell in some way gave comfort but in another made things worse as I knew the smell would not last for ever and eventually James' natural odour would vanish. We talked about what had happened that day. Samantha spoke with so much hatred and vengeance about the boy who drove the car. I just put it down to emotions running high; our boy had gone and she needed someone to blame as neither of us ever thought James would be taken from us in such a way. I was too upset even to go down that path. Samantha would not let it drop – she had had experience of the lad who was known amongst his peers to be immature and often lied. She kept crying, telling me that she had tried to stop James from getting into the car with him, especially as the lad had only just passed his test. Samantha was talking with fear about how she was not going to be able to carry on and that she had nothing left to live for.

At that time, if I had been asked, I would probably have agreed that James was the reason I worked hard and built up my business. With him gone, what was the point? But I had to be strong for the two of us, knowing that it was my responsibility to try, however hard, to hold things together. Some time passed and Samantha and I eventually faced her friends and I thanked them for their kindness in being there and supporting us. Mark hugged me and was crying as much as me, but for different reasons. James was his mate. Someone he had learned to live with as well as his mum. Samantha was still in such a state that Mark had called the doctor to give her a sedative.

Tempers were frail in Samantha's house when blame was discussed, but this was to be expected. No-one really knew what had happened – everyone was surmising, which was not healthy for Samantha as her mind just went into overdrive. The driver would have this on his conscience and would have to live with it for the rest of his life. At the time I was sure that he must have been devastated that James had died and that his life would never be the same again, just as ours would not. I found the atmosphere in the house upsetting. I was still trying to absorb the fact that James had gone. I did not care at the time who was to blame. I stayed for a while but knew that I had to get back to my waiting family at James' other home in Bearsted, and of course to Louise.

Graham was still on hand to take me back to Bearsted. This time I was ready to go via the accident area as I had to do this at some time. I somehow felt safe with Graham, knowing that he would try as best he could to explain matters as he knew them so far. Most of it was still speculation.

It appeared that James' friend had called for him at around 12.30 pm to go into Maidstone to get a takeaway. He was an inexperienced driver and had had a full driving licence for about eleven days or so. They drove into Maidstone via Wateringbury. This caused us to surmise at the time that maybe the car was speeding entering the corner, possibly hitting a kerb – the driver lost control and swerved across to the other side of the road in front of a car coming in the opposite direction. As James was in the passenger seat, the impact was side on and James was probably killed instantly.

My only thoughts at this time, after speaking with Graham, were: Did James suffer? We later came to learn that there was a passer-by who was a qualified first aider and nurse who stopped within a minute of the accident. She confirmed to us that James had had no pulse and had died on impact. This was the only part of the accident that made me feel slightly better. I would not have wanted him to suffer, especially as neither of us who brought him into the world was there with him when he passed.

We proceeded on to Bearsted.

On arrival in Bearsted I had new emotions all over again with my own family. Many more tears flowed, which I will admit, with hindsight, does make you feel better. They say tears cleanse the soul and I firmly believe this is true. Crying is an emotion that we should all learn to accept and never be ashamed of. I know I did plenty of it.

My family and closest friends were all there and questions were asked as to what had happened but, with no confirmed evidence, we were only surmising. They were all puzzled why this had happened and were finding it hard to accept that James had gone. Nothing like this had happened to any of us before. We'd all had elderly relatives who had died, but never someone so young and so cherished – someone who had his whole life ahead of him.

My father was in pieces. He was inconsolable. James had been his Number One and I was his only son. He was grieving for both of us now: James for a life lost and me for a life changed for ever so dramatically. My father was worried how I would cope in losing James as he knew how close we were. We all just stood in the kitchen in a state of shock. I mentioned that we would have to start thinking about the funeral. My family and friends just sobbed, but I had to get this organised to ensure James' funeral would have been just what he wanted and something to make him proud. My mother had been diagnosed with Alzheimer's some months earlier and we knew a shock like this would only send her into a downward spiral.

Eventually everyone left, still shell-shocked, and I went and sat down in the lounge. In the quietness of the room, you could hear a pin drop. The room was adorned with Christmas decorations as the previous Friday we had put them up, being the first weekend in December. This was the first year James had not helped us. He had had more important business to take care of, such as being out with his mates, but I had sent him a photo of the tree as he loved Christmas. I gazed at the tree with tears in my eyes. We sat motionless for a while, not knowing what to say as there were no words in our minds to talk about what had just happened to us. Our lives had changed forever.

I then mentioned to Louise that I wished James would give me a sign, just to let me know he was OK and not suffering. On the fireplace hung three, tiny stockings in an arch. We stared at them, not saying a thing with the stillness of the night. Just at that moment the middle stocking dropped and fell to the floor. Louise immediately said, "There's your sign." Puzzled, I asked what she meant. Unbeknown to me, Louise had hung the three stockings there – one for each of us and James' stocking had just fallen down. My heart secretly smiled as I knew James was still here with us. I questioned it for a moment and then, after placing it back, it dropped again. It was never to be put up again. It made me feel a little easier in my mind as I took this as a sign from James letting me know he was there with me in spirit, if not in body.

We sat for what seemed like an eternity in the lounge and then we retired to bed. Louise went to our bed, but I went to sleep in James' bed. I needed to feel close to him, lying in his bed with the tee shirt I had taken from the wash basket at the West Malling home snuggled up by my face, allowing his aroma to send me off to sleep eventually.

LEARNING TO MOURN

Louise and I were up early the following morning with not much sleep under our belt. The next day had begun and I was hoping that it was a dreadful nightmare, but alas it wasn't. We drank tea and more tea, as that seemed the only thing left to do.

Our Family Liaison Officer arrived to see how we were and to take us to the accident site to lay flowers. He explained that the driver had been in hospital overnight but that he was still not up to any questioning so we were no further with any answers as to what had happened. Louise asked him if we had to register James' death, but he explained that as it was an accident the police would see that this was done.

By now neighbours who had seen visitors come and go realised, with a police car outside, that something serious was up. They were eventually to find out that morning. Many of the kids that James played with, who were older, were distraught. Flowers were arriving, as well as cards by hand, with many condolences by phone. Graham gave me the name of a family funeral director called Birds. We gave them a ring and I spoke to Darren, the owner, who asked us to come to see him later in the day.

I needed to get James' body released as soon as possible. I wanted the funeral to be arranged within the next five days as I did not think Samantha would make it through the weekend the way she had been talking the night before. She did not even want to come to the funeral. We had to wait for the post mortem to be done. Graham had made it clear how distraught we were and he was hoping the post

29

mortem would be done first thing so that James' body could be released on Monday afternoon, the day after he had died.

My friend Robert arrived with his brother, Mark, and they asked if there was anything they could do. Rob had been in the car with us when we got the news of James' death. With all the emotion I realised that the Golf car I had got James had arrived at the garage and this had to go. I didn't care what they did with it – I could not have it around. They left to sort this out. I was told afterwards that the salesman who dealt with James was distraught as James had been in many times with excitement to show off to his friends the car he was to get. Many thanks go to the Volkswagen dealer in Maidstone who immediately refunded the deposit and cancelled the sale, which they were not obliged to do – but they did out of kindness and sympathy to us. They also were kind enough to send flowers to the house that afternoon as they too were in shock at receiving the news. With the car sorted out, this was one less thing to face.

Louise and I visited Samantha in the morning, and tears and emotions continued to run high. This was the first time that I saw two mothers, one a step-mum, cry together. They comforted each other in the knowledge that James, in his wisdom, had kept his life separate in each household. When he was with his mum in West Malling, James was doing things her way; when he was with his step-mum in Bearsted, he did things our way. Things were talked about, Louise learning what James used to do in West Malling and Sam learning what James got up to in Bearsted. Crying was to become part of a daily routine, but being so fresh we tried to be brave, if that is the word to use.

I would go down and sit in James' bedroom for a while as I had never done this before. You see, Sam never came to our house and I never entered hers. There was an invisible line where we respected each other's privacy living so close. I didn't mind, as I just enjoyed James being in the same area and close to me.

Mark, Sam's partner, was also in a terrible state, blaming himself for letting James get in the car but, as I said, it wasn't anyone's fault that he left that lunchtime.

Sam and I talked for a while and I mentioned that James' new car was now gone. She said he was so excited about the car and it made her cry again. I explained that James was not aware that I had bought him his own number plate and that it upset me to think that he would never know. Sam looked up and glanced at me with a smile I had not seen for ages. Still with tears in her bloodshot eyes, she went on to tell me that James had found the number plates hidden in a spare cupboard and had told her and all his friends that his dad had got him his own number plate. He did know. I then filled up with a different emotion, overcome by a warm feeling that James had secretly found out. I was pleased – it was almost a 'Thank God' feeling.

We continued to look at photos and reminisce. Mark and Louise were in the kitchen as they knew we needed the time together and I am sure they needed their time together as they were feeling the same way but without the blood relationship. Regardless of that, they still loved James just as much. Sam's mum was also there to comfort her.

We got ourselves ready to drive to the accident site. On the way Sam and I talked about the funeral. She had now agreed to come, but Samantha wanted James to be buried. I just could not agree as I had been to burials before and know they are really hard to attend and to see. I did not want this for James. She eventually agreed with me. I knew we would find it hard to ever visit James if he had been buried, as there would always be a feeling of wanting to dig the grave up just in case it had all been a terrible mistake. It sounds stupid, but your mind plays tricks on you in times such as these.

We all arrived at the accident site. We were greeted by a sea of flowers and burnt-out candles from the night before. So many floral tributes and even photos were laid by the roadside. Word had spread fast and people had made the effort to show their respect for him. We noticed that the bend in the road was not a particularly tight bend; in fact, the area where the car had stopped was a long way from the bend.

We laid our flowers for James. Bits of the car lay around our feet – indicators, bulbs, bits of metal. We walked along the road and noticed there were no tyre marks on any of the kerbs. Strange, we thought, but there was no other explanation as to why the car would swerve into the oncoming traffic. We tried to re-enact, in our minds, what could have happened. If the car was travelling at speed and had hit a kerb, there would almost certainly be fresh tyre marks, and surely there should have been skid marks coming off the kerb into the road? But nothing! There were skid marks apparent in the road, but nowhere near the kerb. The car had gone up onto a grass verge and into a ragstone wall and we could see the wall had partly collapsed due to the impact. The grass verge was about a foot high, so the speed of the car must have been quite fast. At this stage we thought we would be unlikely to know what had happened as it seemed to have been an accident.

That afternoon, Louise and I went to the funeral parlour to arrange the funeral. Sam was not up to it – I think she felt that if she had come with us, it would finally be accepting that James had gone. We were advised there was a double funeral available for the Friday so we booked this. We were recommended a double funeral due to the amount of people who wanted to come. We picked the coffin, the casket to hold the ashes, our flowers, what cars would be needed… all still in a state of shock at having to arrange the funeral for my son, but I was determined to remain strong to give James the funeral he would be proud of. I could not and would not let him down.

We went through the days organising different things for Friday. The evenings were the worst. When people had gone home we did not want to put the TV on as it felt like our old life, so we sometimes sat in silence – our thoughts wandering to Friday, to what James was talking about in the car, what would we do at Christmas, never seeing him again. Our minds were like minefields. We did not eat for four days after James died. It is surprising how your body can survive just on tea. Our hunger was suppressed with grief.

That evening I went upstairs and turned on the computer. I signed in on James' password and looked at the music on his iPod. I could see the last tracks that he played, as well as the most-played tracks that he obviously loved. They were tracks that wouldn't usually appeal to me, but they did now. I listened for a while, weeping at the thought of James not being here with me. Little did I realise this thought was so wrong, because he was still with me all the time, as I would come to learn in the months to follow.

I had an email the following day from James' best friend – he was also a James, but known as Lewi to his friends. He informed me that he had a video of James on his mobile phone that every one of his close friends will remember. It captures James' beautiful smile and fantastic personality in only 15 seconds. He stumbled across this video when he was transferring all the pictures and data from his phone to his laptop. Once Lewi had transferred all that he wanted, he deleted everything off the phone. All the pictures and videos were removed apart from the one of James. All it kept saying was, "File not supported – cannot remove data." Still, to this day, he cannot work out why this was the only file that could not be deleted. Lewi told me he always wonders if it's James saying, "No matter what memory I am in, I will never leave you." It will be kept forever.

The next day people continued to drop in flowers and tributes. Many did not stop as they just did not know what to say or even how to say it. I spent many hours just staring into space, sitting in the lounge wondering if I should take the Christmas tree down or not. I certainly did not light it. I didn't want to. It wasn't right or it appeared not to be. It was just the way my mind was working overtime. Putting on the lights seemed a way of celebrating Christmas and I just did not want to even think about the day. Should I take the tree down or leave it up? I knew that James loved the tree, which we had had for years, so maybe leave it up but leave the lights off? This is what I decided to do.

On 6th December we were advised that James had been placed in the Chapel of Rest. I had arranged with Sam to collect some of the clothes that James liked as well as some of his personal items. We arranged to meet Sam and Mark at the funeral parlour so that we could all see James together for the first time since he had died. The clothes had been given to Darren, who had arranged for these to be placed on James before we saw him. Arriving at the Chapel of Rest, we were all anxious, not really sure what to expect or how we would react. Everyone's emotions were all over the place, emotions we had never experienced before.

We all went in together to see James; all of us nervous as we were not sure how he was going to look. We were all crying as we walked in. Sam immediately said it was not James lying there. She meant it did not look like James as all life had been drained from his face. Of course, I did not see this as I thought he looked at peace. Everyone saw him in a different way.

I was annoyed as the bandage was still in place over James' face. I questioned Darren. He looked directly at me and said, "There was nothing we could do and the bandage was the only way of covering up the damage to James' face." Little did I know at the time, that this was where the impact had occurred. James' face appeared bruised. I couldn't understand it as I thought James would be back to his usual appearance – I did not realise that on a dead body blood comes to the surface after some time.

After going back into the Chapel of Rest, I sat with James talking, hoping that he could hear me. I kissed his hand and held it for a few moments. To be honest, when you see a loved one lying there, part of you feels as if they are going to sit up, as if it is a sick joke. It all felt so strange. James was now cold and the expression on his face had changed. It was totally different from when I saw him in the hospital but that was only to be expected. I kissed him goodbye and knew that this was not going to be the last time I went and saw him.

Darren came in and asked if I wanted a lock of James' hair. I asked him for four, one each for me and Sam, and one each for the grandparents. This was very important, to keep safe for as long as I lived. As hair never dies, it would be the one thing of James' being that I could keep for ever knowing it would never change.

We finalised the funeral arrangements. I agreed with Sam that James should leave from West Malling first, and then come to Bearsted to leave from his other home as he treated both homes the same. Darren agreed and said it was a good idea: it had never been done before, but he felt it was best option under the circumstances. Flowers were next on the agenda. We decided that we would spell the name 'JAMES' in flowers, pink ones. James liked pink. Then flowers from Mark and Louise in different designs. A teddy bear shape was agreed upon amongst others. Many people think flowers are a waste of money but we could not even think about that – we just wanted James' funeral to be bright and fresh, just like him.

Afterwards none of us felt like we wanted to go straight home so we all walked down the road and had a drink in the local pub. This was to be the first time all four of us sat together talking just about the good times with James and what he had got up to. We all recalled some good memories, and each learned of new ones as James always kept his life with Sam and me separate. The moment we sat down, a song came on by Shanice – 'I Love Your Smile.' We looked at each other and agreed that this was appropriate as James always smiled. I felt this was another sign from James, acknowledging we were all together. A lump was in my throat but I was determined not to cry. We had a few drinks and left to go our separate ways once again. We all drew comfort from each other as even though we all had our own friends, most of them had children so they could never understand what we were going through, having lost our child. Only the four of us knew James inside out and the four of us were united in grief.

The following days were, as you can imagine, worse than ever as the funeral day approached. Arrangements had been made to have the wake at the Tudor Park Hotel, Bearsted, which was kindly arranged by Robert and Mark. They took care of everything, food and drink, and they even arranged the portrait of James that was in his bedroom to be on show in the entrance. Louise, who was stronger than me, did the service book, arranging the photos and putting the whole thing together. Sam and I had chosen the hymn and the intro music from James Blunt – 'High' followed by 'You're Beautiful' as

James was given over to rest. All went to the printers – his grandad's printers of course – and now all we needed to do was wait for the day to arrive. I also received a call from James' school, Sackville, inviting us to the last Wednesday church service before Christmas, which would be dedicated to James. I accepted but spoke to Sam who was not keen, so I asked Mark if he would like to accompany me, to which he agreed.

We arrived at the school church to be greeted by Mrs Sinclair, James' headmistress. She said that the service, the last of the term, was dedicated to James with many short readings. As James always enjoyed these, extra were added. Some of his classmates would read. When Mark and I entered the church, we were taken to the front pew. We sat down waiting for the school pupils to arrive and admired the church interior and the strong lights which were shining down on us. These were halogen lamps: very bright. As I gazed around, Bang! I jumped, as I had no idea what I had just heard. The two halogens had both gone out. I smiled at Mark and said that was James letting us know he was there. I could feel him.

The service went well and I thanked Mrs Sinclair for dedicating it to James. She mentioned that next year in the spring there would be a tree-planting in the school grounds in remembrance of James and that we would be invited to attend the planting. We said our goodbyes and left with a smile, thinking that James would have loved the service. It was a shame that Sam had not been up to it. Mark had said that she was not feeling good and was struggling with the loss, as we all were. I felt I had to support everyone for James but it was difficult as no two people ever grieve in the same way.

We visited Sam and Mark on and off throughout the week just really to support each other. One morning we arrived and Sam was fuming, to say the least. The driver of the car at the time of the accident had been released from hospital and had gone straight to the local pub. Mark had shot round there to find that he had left, but this we found out was how his life was to continue where ours had ended. This behaviour was relayed to the police, who asked the driver and his family to try to stay clear of Sam and Mark over the coming weeks and not to go to the funeral as it would cause bad feeling.

Sam was still distraught that James had died and the driver had just walked away from the accident. She wrote him a letter begging to know what had happened but heard nothing, not even a letter of condolence. Sam's mum then wrote, but unfortunately the driver's parents reported Sam and her mum to the police for harassment. The police explained that the driver's parents had been told not to make contact, but why report Sam for harassment? It was obvious she was a distraught mother grieving for her son. I, at this stage, still wanted to believe it had been an unfortunate accident that could not have been avoided as I had to channel my emotions elsewhere and get through Friday.

The next couple of days were really bad. I visited James every day as I just did not want him to be lying there alone. My father came down as I had persuaded him to see James. At first he was reluctant, but after taking Dad there to say his goodbyes he felt much better for having seen James. We all knew how very much my father loved James and missed his phone calls. My mum went in a day later to be with James alone. She preferred this as she was coping a lot better than my father. He was still inconsolable to the point where no-one could talk to him about James, not even about the good times we had all had together. Time had come for the last goodbyes, person-to-person so to speak, so I had the last five minutes with James before the funeral the next day.

Flowers had already started to arrive and the letters spelling out 'JAMES', that we had ordered, were there. I smiled as I walked out, thinking James would love the pink roses and carnations that spelt his name. Returning home and sitting once again in the lounge in silence was all I could do at this time. Nothing mattered any more. The worst day was yet to come.

That night I received a phone call from Mark. One hundred plus of James' friends from home, school, college and even the pub had decided to walk to the crash site to lay flowers, candles and letters and to hold a silent vigil there for James. I was overwhelmed by their thoughtfulness. The police had to shut the road off for their own safety as there were so many of them. I cried tears of pride that he was so well liked and that people cared so much for him to do this: they had all united in their grief for James. This small gesture spoke volumes in my heart and I realised from that moment that none of James' friends would ever forget him, especially as he was taken from them so young – in his prime. Teenagers are much more open with their feelings than when I was younger. I knew that they loved James and that he had loved them.

Louise went to the accident site again with Nic and her sister, Tracey, whom James had known since he was a young boy. By now the mass of flowers had grown, along with candles, fluffy toys and even a bottle of Coke, as James always drank this in the pub. Louise stopped to read all of the cards from our friends, James' friends and neighbours, and an arrangement of lilies caught her eye. The card read, "Sorry mate it ended this way," with the name of the driver and his girlfriend on the card. Louise was livid – not because the flowers had so obviously not been chosen by him but to have such cold words on a flower arrangement, left by the person who was driving the car that killed James, was just too much. She felt it degraded his resting place. Louise took the flowers from the roadside and asked Nic to throw them in her bin when she got home. Upon arriving home, Louise relayed to me what had happened. I was angry with her for taking the flowers as I felt James' resting place had been disturbed, but the more and more I thought about it, I realised she was right to remove them. None of us wanted them there. We felt it tarnished James' death by having these words placed on the site where James had died. Close friends of his had left cards with their feelings on – but 'Sorry it ended this way'? My life as I knew it had ended this way; James' family's life had ended this way; it was as if he had run over an animal in the road. Maybe I was being overly sensitive – perhaps this was the only way he could deal with it… but I can only say what I felt.

During the visit to the accident site, the girls got talking and Tracey mentioned a medium that her friend had visited, if I was interested. Louise had always believed in mediums and the after-life, but I had never had any reason to really question it to decide what I believed. The medium stuck in Louise's mind as Tracey mentioned she had brought a child through for Tracey's friend. Nothing more was said about it until later …

THE FUNERAL

I could not sleep much the night before the funeral as I was on edge most of the time. I had visited James the day before just before they closed his coffin – that made it seem so final as I could never physically see him again. Coming downstairs that morning was horrible, knowing what was to come. We were really in limbo – dreading the day ahead but wanting to put James to rest.

Flowers were already turning up with more cards. By now we had the whole dining table full of letters and cards from all over the world, including Dubai, New Zealand and America, from friends and customers. One of the cards simply said, "There are no words in the English dictionary to describe what has happened," and this was so true. One of my neighbours, Liz, whose boys used to play with James, had very thoughtfully gone and spoken with builders who often parked in our road whilst erecting houses nearby to refrain from doing so and to stop the use of any machinery between 9.30 and 11.00 as a mark of respect. They carried out her wishes, which seemed such a simple thing, but had we had to see James off to the noise of a pneumatic drill, it would have overshadowed the whole day. I was grateful for their respect.

My parents and sisters arrived early to show support and bring the flowers with them. Dad had a large display fashioned like a mobile phone, in blue, with James' photo as the picture on the phone screen. Although it looked good, it wasn't something that was appreciated at the time as all I could think of by now was the arrival of James.

I paced up and down the lounge for what seemed like hours, but was probably only 20 minutes or so. My friend John arrived and gave me a hug. As the minutes moved on, I knew that soon the cars were going to turn the corner. A few moments later they did. We all moved out of the house dreading getting into the cars and dreading seeing the main hearse parked there with James inside. I broke down on the driveway and Louise just held me. There was nothing she could say as there were no words of comfort at that time.

Graham Parlour, our Police Liaison Officer, arrived with the cars. Sam, Mark, Sam's mum and her step dad were already in one car and we had the one behind James. The police car was in front of the hearse as it was to lead the way. Tears were rolling down my cheeks as I saw the coffin smothered in beautiful flowers with James' name on the side. We got in the car all numb from grief. No-one said anything. It did not feel right, James lying in the back of the hearse. There was just the sound of quiet sobbing.

As we started off, Darren walked in front of the hearse, in the usual way, as the police car moved on. Darren got back in the hearse and we set off down the road. I commented how James would be pleased to have been in a new Volvo hearse that Darren had just taken delivery of. I thought, 'Typical!' When we approached the first junction, we saw that Graham had parked the police car at an angle so no traffic could pass, and as we turned the corner, he saluted James. I was so proud and impressed that Graham had thought to do this. It made me go all cold. Everyone commented on it and started to sob.

Graham continued to overtake the procession of cars with his flashing blue light. He stopped traffic at every roundabout or junction, which made James look so important and special, which he was. There are not many people who have a police escort to their final resting place, and for a short time it took away some of the pain to think Graham had made James' journey respectful and special. As a young boy, James was obsessed with police cars and blue flashing lights and now ironically he had his own police escort, a salute, traffic being stopped on his behalf and blue flashing lights.

The journey to the crematorium took us around 20 minutes. As we turned the corner into the crematorium, which had a long drive up to the entrance, we saw a sight we never expected to see – there was a sea of people lining the road as we drove up slowly, all looking down as a mark of respect for James and for us. James would have been in his element – there was a brand-new Maybach, Bentleys, Rolls-Royces, BMWs, Range Rovers – you name it, all James' favourite cars were there.

People had really made the effort for him. There were hundreds of people – around 400 I was told afterwards. It was amazing. School buses from two of James' schools had turned up, plus people from the college where he had only been for several months. This was incredible. I was overcome with people's outpouring of grief and respect. As the cars pulled up, I started to recognise people.

We all got out and waited for some of James' best mates to carry James in, with us following. How these boys must have felt. It would be something they would live with for the rest of their lives, having to cremate one of their friends at such a young age. I really felt for them that day but was so pleased they had all accepted our request for them to carry their friend in. The music from James Blunt 'High' started playing and in we went, all of us on autopilot.

It took some time for the people to settle down. Being so many, there were speakers set up outside the crematorium so that the large majority who could not get inside were able to be a part of the service. When this got underway, it was extremely difficult. I just looked forward. I couldn't face looking behind and catching someone's eye as I might have crumbled and not been able to get up and do my tribute to James. The first hymn was sung: it came and went. I couldn't really concentrate on the hymn, knowing I had to get up soon afterwards. When it came to it, I was composed as I realised that I was not going to fail in what I had to say. After all, you do not get another chance. This was it.

I got up and approached the podium with my tribute, laid it on the podium and started. In reading, you could say that I was oblivious to who was there and even where people were sitting. I kept my strength, occasionally pausing to pull myself together.

My speech was as follows:

James, what can I say? You were a son to be proud of and it was such a pleasure and a privilege to call you my son. You were loved so much. You were always polite, courteous and caring. You never had a bad bone in your body. You matured into such a lovely boy who lived his life to the full and beyond. With your cheeky smile, you knew that we would never say no... well, only five times, before we eventually said, "Yes." When you came home wearing your earring for the first time, I'll be honest, I was none too pleased, but as usual, that smile won me over and I had no choice but to agree. And I am glad I did.

Whether it be an iPod, the latest phone, computer, golf clubs, fishing equipment or the odd label or two – that smile won every time.

Mobile phones. James had a bigger stock of Nokia phones than Carphone Warehouse. If there was a GCSE in Nokia phones and phone calls, James would have passed with honours. After months of negotiation with Vodafone, we tried to achieve a tariff that allowed him free texts and free calls. But oh no, James exceeded every tariff! In the end, Vodafone agreed that the best way forward was to allow all the phones on the company contract to have free calls to one another. However, James did not seem to realise that his friends were not on that tariff. A new phone was just... a phone call away. James' advice on the latest phone was always sought from his cousins, Emily, Katie, Jamie and Daisy, as James was their hero.

I used to talk to James twice or more a day. Apart from him telling me how his day was going, it would always be, "Dad, have you seen this?" and "Dad, have you seen that?"

But at the end of every call, without fail, James always told me that he loved me. Every time that I picked him up or dropped him off, even in front of his friends, we would always kiss, and part with the same line, "Love you."

James had such a full life. He travelled the world on holidays with both his mum and Mark and Lou and I, sometimes having two summer holidays a year.

At this point I would like to thank Mark for being a great mate to my son.

James had two wonderful homes where both his bedrooms had the same interior colours, beds, furniture... and boxer shorts on the floor.

James loved his music and spent many hours downloading songs for his iPod, causing me to upgrade the computer many times, especially when there were 2,343 songs in total, which is nearly seven days' worth of continuous play. This amounted to 9.1 Gigabytes which, I am told, is unbelievable!

James' latest craze was eBay, buying and selling, wheeling and dealing, just like me and his grandad. I am in no doubt that James would have made his way in the world... had he been allowed to.

James was always insistent about what he'd wear: designer clothes and trainers. He was most particular about gelling his hair before leaving the house.

James loved all of his family and friends and even found love himself. His friends were everything to him, with him joking about, playing tricks and just being James.

We have come to realise that James was everything to his friends. Meeting so many of them on Wednesday night at The Spitfire, I learned so much more about how he was a joy to be with, making people laugh all the time.

I also found out that so many older people had a lot so much respect for James, given his age. I have no doubt, James, that where you have gone, you will make many new friends, keeping them entertained just as you did in this life.

James, your mum and I were always proud of you, especially when you passed your GCSEs, which did come as quite a shock as no revision seemed to be taking place. I do not think MSN run revision courses online! You even won the school fishing trophy.

He was obviously well thought of by everyone as Sackville School have had a memorial service in memory of James, this week, which I attended. A tree-planting will take place in the spring at James' previous school, Radlett Prep in north London.

At the age of 14 James gave me the honour of being my best man when I remarried, in September 2003. He was so proud and conducted himself immaculately throughout the day. James looked good in his morning suit… and he knew it.

In September this year, after nagging his grandad and taking me, his mum and his nan, backwards and forwards to the garage, we finally ordered James' car. The colour choice had to be perfect, as did the wheels, stereo and spoiler. James was so excited, he would tell everybody. I have only just learned that James even found out, whilst exploring the house for Christmas presents, his surprise number plates: JB 55 JJB. James once again added a few more numbers to the Vodafone bill and most people in Kent knew within hours!

I am so sorry that James never got to drive the car. I retained his personalised number plate JB 55 JJB and maybe one day will place it on a car.

So many people have been affected by James' death. It gives us all comfort to know how much he was loved by us all and we are so pleased that his smile, his laughter and cheekiness gave us all so much pleasure. We have been overwhelmed by the tributes to James that we have received. I have been fortunate in having the best, loving, father/son relationship you could ever wish for. We shall all miss James terribly and I know that one day we shall see each other again.

I should now like to read this poem for you:

We can shed tears that he has gone...
Or we can smile because he has lived.
We can close our eyes and pray that he'll come back,
Or we can open our eyes and see all he's left.
Our hearts can be empty because we can't see him
Or we can be full of the love we shared.
We can turn our back on tomorrow and live yesterday
Or we can be happy for tomorrow...

because of yesterday.
We can remember James, and only that he has gone
Or we can cherish his memory and let it live on.
We can cry and close our mind,

be empty and turn our back
Or we can do what he'd want –
Smile, open our eyes, love and go on.

The joy and happiness James brought into our lives, and all the wonderful memories we hold, will be with us for ever.

James, when we said goodbye we always kissed and said we loved each other. So I say to you now, "Goodbye (blow a kiss), and… Love you!"

I tried to make the speech in part light-hearted as that was how James would be remembered by many of his friends. I did not want to make it morbid as this was not James: it was not how he lived his life and it would not be fair to all the young people there who had probably never been to a funeral before, let alone a funeral of one of their best friends. I continued through the whole speech keeping my emotions in check, almost robotic as I knew if I started to cry I would not have been able to continue.

I didn't really notice people's reactions to the speech and, to be honest, I didn't care. I paid the tribute for James, as my final words to him whilst he lay in front of me. Mark did a tribute after me and two of James' friends got up and spoke about him. They laughed about how, whenever they were out, they knew they never had a chance of pulling any girls as all the girls flocked over to James. What respect they showed for James by being able to stand up and share this observation with over 400 people. I laughed to myself, knowing that's exactly how James would have been.

The service continued but I could not take it in. All I could see was James lying in front of me.

After the committal the curtains drew and 'You're Beautiful', by James Blunt, played over the loudspeaker. This was the worst bit of the whole week. It was so final. Part of you wants to prise open the coffin and give your son one last cuddle, and part of you wants him to be at peace. I sobbed as the final gap in the curtains disappeared. There was no going back now. Louise and I just hugged and cried, quietly sobbing into each other, knowing we would never see James again.

When the vicar nodded, we started to make our way out to the back of the crematorium where all of James' floral tributes had been laid out. I was told that in order for the amount of people to come in and through the chapel they had to play 'You're beautiful' five times.

Outside I now started to see the sea of flowers and people who had come to pay their last respects. The flowers were unbelievable. There were 200 plus tributes from all over. We never really got a chance to see all of them but all the cards were later taken and put in an album for us by the funeral directors. We stood around for what seemed ages and, after looking at all the flowers and speaking to as many people as I could, we left to go to the hotel where we had laid on some food and drinks. I had decided in my own mind that I was going to come back in the morning and have a quiet moment to myself and look at the flowers once again.

There were people at the funeral that I had not seen for years and acquaintances from work that I never expected to be there. Up to eight months later I was still hearing of people talking about James' funeral who I did not even know were there.

The mood in the car on the way to the hotel had lifted as we all felt James had been laid to rest, and to be honest, it was a relief that we had all got through the service without crumbling. Don't get me wrong: we cried and sobbed throughout the whole service but we felt we had done James proud.

The gathering at the hotel was hard but after a few stiff drinks it became easier, as I knew James would not want me to sit in the corner and be depressed. After all, this in a way was a celebration of James' life – and what a life he had had.

I was now able to see different people and meet some of James' friends for the first time. There were so many. One of James' best friends, Lewi, came to see me for a quiet word.

"Before we start, James didn't owe you money, did he?" I joked, with a smile on my face.
"No," said Lewi, "I want you to promise me something."
"Sure," I replied.

49

"James and I made a pact that when he got married I was to be his best man and when I get married he would be mine. Well, I am now asking you to fulfil James' part and be my best man when the time comes." I was honoured and said that if he changed his mind in the future I would step down. This was not going to happen, Lewi said.

Lewi sent me a letter after James died and it seems appropriate to include it here:

> "I have had some of the best days of my life with James, so many memories that will never be forgotten. Even though he may not be here in person any more, his wicked sense of humour and awesome smile that even Tom Cruise would have died for, lives on. James will always be my best friend – even though he is not here, his personality is irreplaceable. There is never a day when we didn't speak on the phone or in person. To have someone like that taken away is very hard to deal with, and when all you can keep hold of is pictures and videos they become more special every time you see them."

The afternoon following our time at the crematorium went very fast, which was good in one way and sad in another. As I turned to walk towards the bar in the hotel to get a stiff drink, Paul, one of my closest friends, approached me. Paul had been responsible for lending me the new Range Rover that James so loved. He said that the Range Rover Supercharge had been put in the storage hangar for me to decide if I wanted the car. This was what James had wanted and Paul said that it would stay there until further notice as no-one was going to drive it until I had made my decision. As Paul walked away, I had already made that decision. I was going to have the car as that is what James had wanted me to have. I didn't care what the cost was going to be. Why should I care now? James was gone. What was I going to do? Save and save for a rainy day? None of us know what's round the corner, so I decided there and then that I would take each day as it came. I was going to drive that car, with James hopefully sitting with me in spirit, in the passenger seat.

People started to go but we just didn't want to leave. We wanted to share in our grief as it seemed to make it easier. My family and close friends, and Sam and Mark, decided we would go to James' favourite pub – somewhere where neither myself nor any of my family had ever been before, yet we had heard so much about it from James. We went there for a couple of hours and then finally went back home to a very quiet house.

I sat in the lounge till it was time for bed when I eventually went to sleep, thinking about James and where he was. He was around, I was now sure of that.

LOOKING FOR ANSWERS

Years ago I had seen a film staring Robin Williams called 'What Dreams May Come'. I decided I really wanted to see it again as it was all about where we go when we die and I thought it would make me feel better if I knew James had gone to the same place. Louise and I went into Maidstone to buy it. Being so near to Christmas, the Salvation Army were playing Christmas carols in the High Street and the whole experience made me on edge. I just wanted to buy the film and get out, back to the sanctuary of our home. There was Christmas all around us – parents shopping with their children, people rushing around merrily. But I did not want any part of it. Understandably so. I was not in the mood for celebrating. We found the film, the last copy in the shop, bought it and went home.

Louise and I revisited the crematorium to see the flowers. There was an abundance of displays lying everywhere. In part, I felt sorry for the others who had their cremations on the same day as James' as his flowers took over the whole forecourt. By now the cards had been taken so we were unable to see which displays were from whom. We had forgotten to take our camera so Louise dropped me off at home and went back to take some photos so we would always have them as visual memories of the day and the respect people gave to James. When Louise returned to the crematorium, a woman came over and asked who the flowers were for. The lady said she had lost her daughter years ago, and when Louise asked if the grief ever gets easier, she replied, "No!"

We watched the film that evening. A lovely film but so sad: we cried our eyes out. The true emotion of the film really came through and the colours of heaven were so vibrant, a place where you would want to be. The film is about a couple who are devoted to one another but due to tragic circumstances the son and father are killed. The mother is so distraught that she commits suicide, believing she has nothing to live for and believing she will meet with them again. But it is not as easy as this. Robin Williams' character goes on a journey to bring the whole family together again in heaven. The film was heart-breaking but gave me comfort in that there was a chance I might see James once again, not in this lifetime but when I die. The film set off the floodgates again and we quietly snivelled on the sofa thinking of James.

Whilst in Maidstone earlier that day, Louise had suggested buying some books written by mediums as I had now expressed an interest in seeing one in the hope they might be able to make contract with James. In Waterstone's we found the appropriate section and noticed that one of the mediums, Mia Dolan, was from the Isle of Sheppey where Louise was originally from, about twenty miles from our house. We decided this was fate so bought all her books. Louise started reading them that evening and she read out the parts that she thought would be a comfort to me.

I was mesmerised, completely hooked and needed to know more. Louise found the books overwhelming as they were written with such truth, describing the emotions Mia felt at losing her son at a young age, how she coped with it and how she helped other people cope with their loss. If only I could get to see Mia, it would be a dream come true. I felt a connection with Mia that I could not explain. Louise finished the first book that evening and ploughed through the others, not able to put them down as they offered such comfort. Mia had been through the loss of a child herself and had helped so many others who had lost children. I now decided I wanted to see a medium. If there really was an after-life, I needed to know as then I would know James was OK. I often panicked that, as he had died so young, he would be in heaven all on his own. A very naïve thought, I now know, but as a father who had just lost his son, I needed to know James was OK and that he was being looked after.

The following day we called into Sam's as the police had requested a meeting with us to discuss the accident. We were not expecting much, to be honest, as Louise and I genuinely thought that it was a pure accident and one that could not have been avoided. Sam was convinced that the boy who had been driving had killed James deliberately to save his own skin, but I did not believe this for a minute. When the police arrived, we were shocked to hear what they had to say. It appeared that the car was speeding and that charges were soon to be brought against the driver. There were no explanations as to what caused the crash: no tyre marks on the curb, no sign of anything running out in front of the car such as a fox or a cat, which the driver was alleging. There was not a cat within a mile of the accident site and foxes rarely stray onto main roads in the middle of the afternoon.

The police assumed the driver had been fooling around but now needed to prove it. They mentioned that they would possibly be charging him with reckless driving. Reckless? What an understatement! Looking into things later, it appears there is no great penalty for causing death by reckless driving; it is simply a fine at most. The police explained this was going to be a long-drawn-out case which was to go on for 15 months or so as they were not allowed to bring it to trial if they thought they did not have enough evidence. We were hopeful that justice would be done.

Sam was bitter, as was I, but as the boy lived so near to her, it was much more difficult for Sam than it was for me. To say she hated him would be putting it mildly. She stopped driving past his parents' house as she could not bear to see them sitting there watching the telly and doing all the normal family things of which we had now been robbed.

The question of insurance documents came up during our meeting as the driver had still not produced his insurance to the police, despite many requests. We were asked to be patient with the time it would take for the case to come to trial, and we were assured that if we ever had any questions, then we should contact the police. They asked us for a list of people who we knew had been lied to by the driver in the past, as the police wanted to build up a character profile of him. Where were we to start? Should we put forward our friends' names too? They had been told by this young man that he had lung cancer. Should we list ourselves, as the driver had told us he had been stabbed at Brixham train station and was fighting for his life? The list was endless.

After the police had left, Sam gave me a book that James' friends had brought round. This contained special messages from all his friends in the area, with some poems, as well as some kind words which made us both very sad but proud that people had thought so much about him. I recall one page in particular that was from one of James' friends who was, in the past, prone to taking drugs. It appeared that James had convinced him that it was not a good idea and made him give up. His words were very touching as his parents had added comments that, if James had not made their son see sense, he might still have been in a bad state. They will always remember him for what he had done. The words that some of James' friends wrote were so emotional. The book was a treasure to keep and to cherish. I decided to leave the book with Sam.

The Friday came that week and I was now going to collect the car James had wanted me to have. One of the reasons it was special was the fact that he rode in this car with me and that I had a photo on my phone of James in the car. I arrived and Paul took me to the showroom. He knew it was going to be hard but commented that in his opinion it was the right thing to do as James loved the car and so did I. I drove out of the showroom and made my way home listening to the music that was on a CD. 'You're Beautiful' came on and I cried most of the way home thinking how James would have been so proud that I had bought the car. I called my dad and said that I had the car, but he noted that there was a catch in our voices when speaking, as I had done what James had wanted.

When I arrived at the roundabout in Bearsted, the CD system stopped and the display screen searched all the CDs. I could tell it was playing up. After a few moments the CD player reset itself and started playing again. I thought, "That's my James, confirming he is here in the car." As I then turned on the radio the track 'I'm sitting down here but hey you can't see me' was playing. Oh my God, it was definitely James. I cried once more, happy that I had received his sign. If the CD had not gone wrong I would not have turned on the radio. This was James' way of making sure it was turned on at the right moment. I checked with Paul, as he had often driven the car, but he confirmed he had not had a moment's problem with the CD player. I was right, it must have been James. I never had a problem with the CD again from that day forward.

That weekend was very quiet and Louise and I just sat in the lounge with no TV on, talking about James and reading more books on mediums and women who had lost children. I could never find any books by fathers who had been through similar circumstances to me. That evening, the light by where I sat started to flicker. I took this as another sign as this light bulb, to this day, has not been changed. I have to admit that I was still comforted by sleeping in James' bedroom as this made me feel closer to him. The smell on his jumper was fading fast and I now felt it was time to be put away. Louise was not at all worried where I slept as long as it helped me. I continued to sleep in James' bed for the next five months. The sun always comes in at the back of our house, directly into James' bedroom. In the lead up to the summer it got so hot in there that I could no longer sleep so moved rooms. I also felt this was the right time; I no longer needed to sleep in James' bed to feel closer to him. I knew he was with me.

On the Sunday after the funeral, we went to our local church. I don't know why as we had never been to a regular service there before, only to carols at Christmas. Whilst there we decided we would offer to donate the church Christmas tree this year and spoke to the vicar. He was aware of our situation, as were many in the church that day. He had said a prayer for James during the service. The vicar was most understanding and the arrangements were made. We had not been particularly religious but the support of the vicar really helped us as he often called round to make sure we were OK.

The tree was put up the week before Christmas and Louise and I were invited to decorate it and place a star on the tree with James' photo on it. Louise made the star with James' photo on and it was the biggest on the tree. He'd have loved that. There would also be a dedication plaque at the bottom of the tree. We were looking forward to doing this and agreed that we would light our own tree on Christmas Eve, which is when I felt it was right.

Louise and I attended the carol service on the Sunday, with my parents and my sister, Debbie. During the quiet prayer time, a glass bauble fell off the tree, hit the concrete floor but stayed intact and rolled towards us. We all looked at each other with a smile on our faces. All of us had been saying a prayer in our minds for James and he had just acknowledged that he had heard them.

On 20th December we had agreed with Sam that James was to have his ashes buried in West Malling churchyard as his friends could visit him there. We decided we only wanted immediate family: Louise and I, Sam and Mark, Mum and Dad, and Sam's mum and step-dad. I arranged for four white doves to be set free: one for my mum and Sam's mum, and one each for Sam and me. The small ceremony was short but still upsetting. Darren, from Birds Funeral Directors, had arranged it all and asked me if I wanted to place the urn in the ground. He explained it would be quite harrowing, but it was something I wanted to do. The release of the doves was wonderful as it felt as if they were taking James to heaven.

With all the ceremonies over we had to now start thinking about how our lives were going to be. The way in which we dealt with matters is really the reasoning behind this book.

THE READINGS

The following week I had decided that I wanted to have a reading to see if I could get some more confirmation that James was near me. I felt he was, but needed the confirmation from a professional medium who could give me an indication that they were really talking with James, or confirmation that there is life after death and that James had not left me totally. I needed to know that I would see James again as this would make my grieving more bearable.

Louise spoke with Tracey, a friend of ours, to get the number of the medium near to us. Her name was Lisa Jayne and she lived about 20 minutes from us. Louise called her. She explained it was a reading for her husband, and Lisa said she would call back to confirm the time. When she did, Louise explained that there would be two of us coming to the meeting which was to be myself and Sam. Lisa said she never gave double readings as they often got confused, but Louise briefly explained the situation and Lisa accepted it was more of a connection we wanted rather than a reading. We were due to go in a couple of days.

We collected Sam and Mark and drove to the address Louise had been given in Cranbrook, Kent. Mark and Louise decided to go for a coffee whilst Samantha and I approached the door which had a sign saying 'Dove Cottage'. The door opened and Lisa welcomed us in. We were very apprehensive at the time but were hoping to hear something. Lisa went into the kitchen for a minute and came back with a smile on her face. She said that she had a young man with the letter J who had been with her all morning and that she had guessed it was for us. All Louise had said to her was that we had recently lost our son – no further details. Louise had been to many mediums before and knew that some of them get as much information as possible before the reading starts only to feed it back to you during the actual session. Louise had given the bare minimum of details over the phone to the point where she said she probably sounded rude and obnoxious! Sam and I glanced at each other.

Lisa commented that the pink jumper I was wearing suited me and that our son was grinning at me. I had only put the jumper on as James loved pink and loved its designer, Ralph Lauren. Then she told us of a car accident and related to us about speed and that James knew nothing and felt nothing when he passed. She described the injuries and the blow to the left-hand side of his head. She said he felt no pain, and that although at first he was shocked at what had happened, he was now fine. Sam started to cry. I was choked but wanted to hear much more to convince myself that James was talking with Lisa.

"Music," Lisa said, "This boy loved his music to the extent that he had many, many songs on his iPod." She asked me to make a CD of James' favourite tracks. She said, "You know, the ones that you listened to the other night." James wanted me to make copies and give them to his friends. Unbeknown to anyone, I had already started making a CD of James' favourite songs. Lisa also said that James' favourite aftershave was red and she could see the name began with his initial J. She then said, "Joop". She was so right.

James then said how much he loved us and knew what good parents we were and all we had given him during his life – he could not have wished for more. James said he was OK and that things would get better in time. I was not to take the tree down but try to accept that he would be there with us. James went on to mention some names of friends, some of which I knew and some known to Sam. It was one of those moments that I did not wish to end, but it did, with Lisa saying that James had to go and that he was hugging both of us with his love.

Lisa took some time to explain some facts that would help us in our time of loss. She was a trained grief counsellor as well as a medium.

We thanked her very much and, as I walked out, I knew I would be back one day. We met up with Louise and Mark and relayed as much as we could remember. I gave Lou a big hug and thanked her for arranging this special morning which gave me hope that James was still with us in spirit. I felt I needed to know more though.

Just before Christmas, Sam wanted to see a medium up north who had been helpful to Holly Well's parents after she had disappeared. Mark and I took Sam up there to see him but she was disappointed with the reading. The medium had told her many things that were true – things about James – but Sam really did not want to hear them. She seemed to be a lost soul floating about in a dark river. She said she believed in the after-life, but this was never enough to lift her head above the dark waters – her grief totally consumed her and Sam constantly cried.

Christmas came along quite quickly. I decided we would continue as normal. Louise's parents were coming round to us on Christmas Day with my mum and dad coming in the evening, to stay the night with my sisters, and their families coming down to us on Boxing Day. Christmas Eve we always had the same routine: Louise and I would walk to Tesco's, grab some last-minute shopping, have breakfast and then always ham, egg and chips for tea. We did exactly the same, as it was what James would have wanted, but the day was subdued. However much I tried though, it was just not the same. It would never be the same again. I absolutely dreaded Christmas Day, my first-ever Christmas without James. Looking back now, I think I was still in shock as everyone commented on how strong I was being, but I didn't feel like it inside.

We got up and quickly opened our presents. We had already bought all the presents before James had died. Usually we take an hour opening all the presents as Christmas is a time we spoil each other, but it was very robotic this year. We unwrapped the present, smiled and put it down; unwrapped the next one, smiled and put it down; the same over and over again.

There was one present left under the tree, a present from Louise to me. I thought she had gone and bought me something expensive but I did not feel that bothered as material things did not matter any more because James was not with me to share them. I opened the present. It was an album. Louise had made a photo memory of James' life: our holidays together; our days out; our wedding; the things James achieved throughout his life. Every beautiful photo of James was under one cover. I cried looking through it as it brought back so many happy memories. It was something to keep forever; something I could take with me wherever I went – and I loved it.

Christmas and Boxing Day came and went and I started to feel as if I needed to see another medium. I had had such a good reading with Lisa that I needed confirmation from someone else that it wasn't a fluke. My sister's friend had recommended someone in Essex who she thought was excellent. We tried calling and calling but never got an answer until one day we decided to be brave and leave a message. It sounds strange but a bad medium really can put you off ever going again, and I needed to have one who had been recommended to me so I would not be misled and lose my ever-growing belief that James was around me all the time.

The lady's name was Sue and she made the appointment for later in the week. The appointment could not have come quick enough. Typically, on the day, the car went wrong. Today, of all days. We could not open the passenger door, and because Louise was driving me to Essex we needed the door to be working, just in case… I drove the car up to London and Paul's team fixed it, so we went to Mum and Dad's for fish and chips! Sue's house was on the route back so everything fitted into place.

We pulled up outside Sue's house. Everything goes through your mind on these occasions, partly caused by nerves, partly caused by adrenalin. What if I had got the wrong day? What if she didn't want to read for me? What if she got it totally wrong? I needn't have worried. Sue greeted me at the door and took me into a small room where she did the readings. She gave me a notepad to make any notes as she explained I probably wouldn't remember once I got out of there. She made a bit of small talk, probably to relax both me and her. After a while she started telling me things that there was no way she could have known. I had never seen Sue before in my life and she did not know anything about my circumstances, nothing.

The first thing Sue said was that she had an impatient young man waiting for me to arrive. She said he had recently passed, with the letter J for James. I was bowled over. Speechless. Sue said that he was very determined to communicate within such a short time of having crossed over. She was very surprised at the freshness of the passing. She said the same sort of things as Lisa had said, mentioning music and love of clothes. Sue also mentioned some bits about the accident, as well as sadness at everything happening so fast. Family members who had already passed and who were around James were mentioned, which also gave me comfort that he was not alone. Sue mentioned my Uncle Jack who had passed a couple of years previously. There was mention of a dog called Ben, which was our old retriever. She also said that she could see James sitting on the stairs and not being able to see whether the landing went to the left or the right but there were steps in the background. This did not mean anything to me but maybe he sat on the stairs when I was at home. I just did not know and I could not explain it.

There were other family things that were told and I must admit most, if not all, were correct. How did she know these facts? Was James really talking to her? I came away more convinced than ever that he was. The comment about the stairs really puzzled me though, as Sue had said so many correct things. James never sat on the stairs to tie his shoelaces so it couldn't be that – teenagers never undid their laces, they simply struggled to get the trainers on any way possible. I just could not place what she meant.

We drove home and I relayed everything to Louise, who said that it was nice to know that James came through so strongly again. We remained silent during the rest of the hour-long journey as Louise knew I was deep in thought.

When we arrived home, I went up to have a bath. Just as I was about to get in, Louise screamed at me to come downstairs. I ran downstairs and there she was holding a photo. "Look!" she exclaimed. I looked at the picture and to my amazement I saw James sitting on the stairs with our landing behind him as described earlier. Looking at the photo, you would not know if the stairs went to the right or the left. This was what the medium was referring to. This was the photo of James he had shown her, with him smiling, which was taken last Christmas. I was so happy that we had made contact once again. I was sure that this was just the beginning as I was going to make it my goal to get back in as close contact as possible to James. I immediately got on the phone and relayed everything to Sam.

I started to work on James' CD which Lisa had mentioned in her reading. I went onto the computer and pulled off the 12 most played tracks and burnt them onto a CD. I made 100 copies. As my father's company was a printers, we produced a sleeve with the picture of James sitting on the stairs, and on the back listed all the titles of all the tracks. We had ordered the cases and I had decided to distribute them at the local pub in Kings Hill where all of James' mates gathered. They all went along and many of the guys agreed that the tracks were perfect and that James would have approved.

I noticed that behind the bar they were collecting donations for James, to give to me. Donations also came from our dear neighbours. It was agreed that with the donations made, which were hundreds of pounds, we would buy two benches with plaques on. One would be at the pub, in the garden, and one would be placed on Bearsted Green opposite the pond. We asked the Parish Council, who were only too pleased to have another bench on the Green. These were ordered. One of the donations was from an elderly gentleman who was always in the pub, sometimes alone, as the crowd was usually quite young. He had donated £50 and when asked why so much, as he seemed by no means able to afford this amount, he said that every time James came into the pub he would always talk to him, no matter whom James was with. The gentleman appreciated that and said he would miss James' smile dreadfully. I was proud, once again, of my son.

Sitting on the bench in Bearsted

Work was not on my mind at this time as we had our guys holding the fort, so to speak, and all was well. Louise would go in from time to time. After the Christmas holidays, we had our annual Boat Show starting on 5th January. I had decided that Fridays were going to be my day where I would not work but attend to James' grave, placing fresh flowers every week. I would use all different colours in the letter 'J'. I was fortunate to have met up with a flower importer who agreed to sell me the flowers each week. He was based only a few miles away and was pleased to assist.

Every Friday was to be James' day. I would stand at his grave and tell him about my week, almost waiting for a reply. I got to know the people at the church, the gardeners and the people with lost ones who were near to James, each one with their own tragic story. I would tend to his grave, do the flowers and then go home and do things like wash the car, play his music – anything James used to love doing. He could always clean a car. Maybe he had had a good teacher!

The more and more we read about the after-life, the more comfort I got in the knowledge that James was well and happy. I started to watch mediums on TV, like Colin Fry and John Edwards, and every reading I heard was similar to my experience. All people were looking for was confirmation that their loved ones were looking over them and that they were OK. When I heard some of the stories, I realised how, in a way, we were fortunate to be able to identify James' body and to give him a proper funeral. Some people never got that chance and I wondered how they would ever find comfort or even a little bit of closure.

Signs

I read a book by a mother who, when she felt her lost son was around her, would always find a pure white feather. I started to get exactly the same signs. Feathers would appear from nowhere – perhaps one in the house, just appearing as James was on my mind, or if I was having a particularly bad day, trying to accept that he was no longer with me. I would get in the car and a pure white feather would be lying on the bonnet. I would go to the crematorium and a trail of white feathers would lead me from the car to the grave. These were not coincidence or feathers from a distraught bird escaping from the clutches of a cat; they were always the same size and always the same colours – pure, brilliant white. The feathers appeared from nowhere to place themselves before me. We would be sitting with friends in the garden and a white feather would float down from nowhere. Pure coincidence, you may think, and maybe it was, but it gave me comfort. They started to appear more and more regularly. I would talk to James at the graveside telling him how much I missed him and loved him, and a single white feather would float down. It happened too often to be coincidence and I saved every single one in a jar in the kitchen.

From time to time I would go to see Sam and have a coffee to reminisce about James and what he might have been doing if he were still here.

We had to order the stone for the grave. This was hard but needed to be done as it took several months to make. Sam chose a book shape with some nice words, which we ordered. Sam wanted to pay for this herself. I of course agreed as it seemed to make her feel better. She was still finding it incredibly hard to accept he had gone and she seemed to be getting worse and worse. She was still on medication from the doctor and it worried me because, whilst it calmed her down and made her sleep, she never really grieved properly for James. Each time she felt a wave of grief coming over her, Sam would take a pill. She still sobbed for James, almost uncontrollably, as she had nothing to occupy her mind, and to be honest, she did not want anything to occupy her mind. Sam's grief surrounded her and took a strong hold of her, almost like a disease. She was getting lower and lower to the point where she stopped answering the phone. I had to ring three times, as a code, before she would pick up.

The New Year came and went in a blur. We, of course, wanted no part of any celebrations. We had invited Sam and Mark over to our house for an early evening meal. After the meal we got chatting and Sam asked to see the wedding video from when Louise and I got married as James had played such a big part in the day. This was the last video we had of James which resembled what he was like when he had passed.

Sam sat there watching the best man's speech and we all had lumps in our throats watching James circulating around the room. This evening Sam saw James' room in Bearsted for the first time. She could not get over how much it resembled his room in London where he had lived when we first moved to Kent.

Louise and I were in bed by 9.30 pm having each taken a herbal sleeping tablet to ensure we heard nothing of the New Year celebrations.

From time to time during Christmas and New Year one of us would go into work to check on the building and to make sure everything was OK. For the first time Louise drove the Range Rover into work. I had a Michael Bublé CD in the player with a song he had recorded with the Bee Gees – one song was called 'How do you mend a broken heart?' and it was Louise's favourite. She said she played it and played it on the 20 minute journey into Sittingbourne as the words were so lovely. As Louise neared the office the chorus got louder and louder to the point where she had to turn it down. She put this down to the fact that maybe the stereo allowed for the noise of the engine, so adjusted the volume accordingly. When the car was going faster, it happened again, just as the chorus came on. Again she thought it was the car adjusting. But then Lou pulled up at traffic lights, so the car was at a standstill, and the song again got louder and louder. She laughed to herself, putting it down to James letting her know he was there, probably annoyed she was driving his car and annoyed that she was playing the same song on repeat over and over again. Louise called out to James, telling him she knew he probably didn't like the song but she did, so let her play it! The car moved off, the song repeated over and over again but the volume never once altered again.

James always seemed to be in the car with us. We were driving into work another day and were listening to 'Hung Up' by Madonna. We never really commented on the song until one of us noticed the hands on the clock in the car, which can only be programmed by the car's on-board computer. The hand had starting spinning and spinning and did not stop. We were amazed. Time goes by so slowly... yet our clock was spinning and spinning as if to contradict what the song was saying. We laughed to each other and I knew I would have to set the clock through the computer when we reached the office. With that, the clock stopped at exactly the time it was on my watch.

From what I have learned, time always goes so quickly for those who have passed, but so slowly for those left behind. I would worry that it might be years before I would see James again and that he would be missing me as much as I missed him. However, as time goes by so quickly for those who have passed, what appears to them as minutes, would appear to us as days, months or even years. James didn't miss me – why should he? He could see me any time he wanted, even give me a cuddle, hear what I was saying to him, give me signs to let me know he was there, but I could not reciprocate, so of course my body ached with missing him so much.

After New Year I tried to focus on the London Boat Show to give me something to keep my mind active. I found it terribly difficult going back into work and would often come home early or shut myself in my office. The show started on 5th January, four days before James' 17th birthday. I dreaded his birthday, especially being so close to Christmas.

My parents and sister came down for James' birthday and our local church opened its doors so that we could light a candle for James, say a prayer and see the book of remembrance with his name in. This became a ritual every year. In the evening we were taking Sam and Mark to James' favourite Chinese restaurant near to our house, as we felt that is what he would have loved. We had a nice time but it was just so difficult being in there without James.

We took the day off from the Boat Show and I have continued to do so since as it always falls on James' birthday each year.

The journey to and from the show I dreaded, as every day we would have to go past the site where we first found out James had died, and of course it brought all of the memories of that day back to me. However, I felt I had to face things head-on to make them easier in my mind, so each day slowly became more bearable.

I continued to get my signs at the show. When I was feeling morbid one day, a spotlight blew just above my head – I knew this was him as I knew if James was to give me a sign, the easiest way was to use electricity. This was something else we had read. The electrician came along to change the bulb and was astonished that all of the lights did not trip as they should have done in normal circumstances. I was not surprised at all. James was there, as he had been the previous year.

People always say that if we are to get signs by smell, it would be a fragrance that we would associate with our lost loved ones. Unfortunately, James was renowned for creating the most terrible smells with his flatulence and if we were to smell James near to us, this is often what we would smell. Driving up to the Boat Show one day, going along the A2, Louise and I noticed the most dreadful smell. She blamed me and I blamed her, but we knew it was neither of us as we had passed the stage in our relationship of not admitting to such things. Whenever we travelled up to my parents for Sunday lunch, James would be in the back listening to his iPod and half way into the journey James would fart. Silent, but extremely violent, is the only way they can be described. Of course, when confronted, he always denied it but we knew it was James and this was the sign he was giving us now.

This happened again one evening. I had been out at a meeting all day and arrived home late. Normally I would go upstairs and change into casual clothes before having my tea. Louse dished up the evening meal and after we had finished she went upstairs. At the top of the stairs I could hear her moaning at me for being so inconsiderate, nagging that I could have at least shut the bathroom door to save her gagging. I appeared at the bottom of the stairs still in my shirt and tie and explained that I had not had time to go upstairs and change. It was James again. This smell only came from the bathroom he used; it was in no other room and we do not have a problem with drainage so there was no way I could blame that.

A couple of months after the Boat Show had finished, I decided I felt the time was right to see Lisa again, but this time on my own. I made the appointment and went along for the reading. Again, I had an amazing reading where she confirmed how my grandparents had died, and she was spot on. She told me that James was saying I now had his watch but to hold onto it and never give it away. He said not to worry, that better times were coming and that I had to learn not to worry about him. He also said that Louise needed me more than him so I should concentrate on her. James described us as two old duffers, as we would sit there reminiscing about him, but he wanted us to move on.

I explained to Lisa that I visited his grave every Friday for me, not just for James, but she said he was saying I didn't need to go every Friday. She described the flower arrangements I had left for him that morning and that he would lie with me of a night-time as I slept in his bed. I was with Lisa for an hour and a half, and at the end of the reading James wanted to say Happy Mother's Day to Lou, as this was fast approaching.

Lisa was amazed at the strength at which James came through for such a new passing. She said she had never felt such love between a 'spirit' and the person she was reading for. This was true – I adored James. He was my only son and I spoilt him rotten but he was never a spoilt brat. We always told each other we loved each other and always had a cuddle, up until the day he died. Unlike many teenage boys, he was never afraid to kiss me in front of his friends, as I related in my speech at the funeral, and I would still cuddle him on the sofa when he stayed with us. James never complained. He always felt protected and knew he was loved unconditionally and this love was shining through now. Happy with the reading, I left.

I got on incredibly well with Lisa and felt I could call her at any time if I needed to have confirmation that James was around me. Many people would say they were worried about me relying on a medium and that I had to grieve by myself, but until anyone has been in my situation, it is not possible to know. There is no right or wrong way to deal with grief. Everyone grieves differently – there is no written rule about how you should feel. I was grieving for James in the only way I knew how. I cherished our memories, knowing there would never be any new ones. I did everything I could for him in life and was now doing it for him in his passing. By going to mediums I felt I could be near to James. It was almost like a telephone conversation with him, and each time I went to a medium I was mesmerised by what I was told as each time the different mediums told me what I had been up to, how James died and his relationship to me – the same pattern emerged every time and each time it gave me a quiet inner peace.

I had grieved openly for James. I did not need a medium to tell me how much I loved him; I just wanted to feel close to him again, and if going to a medium helped me to be able to move on, then what did it matter how often I went? I was not going to contest that James had died. I was not looking for answers as to how he died; I just wanted to feel at one with him again.

I now wanted Louise to visit Lisa, just in case James had something else to say to her. It sounds desperate but in the early days I suppose you could say I was desperate for him to make contact and to let me know he was OK. Louise had been to mediums before, quite a number of times, but was more nervous this time as she, too, was desperate to hear from James. Not being a blood relative, Louise was worried that he would not connect with her but James came through straightaway. Again, he said that we had to move on. He said he had had a wonderful, fantastic life and thanked Louise for loving him.

Lisa said she could see Louise crying in a locked bathroom and that James was there with her when she cried. Unbeknown to me, Louise would often go into the bathroom to cry, where I could not see her as she knew I would get upset myself. If I never knew this, how could Lisa possibly know if James was not telling her?

One thing Lisa did tell Louise was that I would become calmer to prepare myself for something coming up in his mum's life. We never really knew what she meant until much later. Lisa understood that we knew James was with us a lot and that he said we should accept things and just move on. Of course, with everything so raw still, this was impossible. However, we had slowly realised that things we could not do in the past were becoming easier. We started to see friends more, nothing too heavy, just meals at each others' houses or the odd meals out.

Louise and I eventually planned a trip to New York with close friends Paul and Pauline. The trip really took our minds off things at home. Paul and Pauline had known James since birth so it was great to reminisce with them. We had a really good time winding each other up, and the girls shopped until they dropped. Years ago we had taken James to New York as he was obsessed with the film 'Home Alone' and the bird lady in the park. I had decided to surprise him one Christmas with tickets – there was not a dry eye in the house as James was totally overwhelmed at the thought of seeing this magical place. I booked us into the Plaza where Macaulay Culkin's character had stayed. We packed our swimming trunks and phoned down upon arrival to see what floor the pool was on. They explained they had no pool; it was made up for the film!

We were in New York for five days and on Day Two we took James to see the bridge in the park where the bird lady fed the pigeons. By ten o'clock that morning James had seen everything he wanted to see and was bored. Looking back, he was too young to go to New York as there is not much for kids to do there. My mum came with us and for the remaining three days he drove us mad with his boredom. I took him to the cinema about three times a day, which he loved, but as soon as the film finished he wanted to know what we were doing next. I was worn out by the time the plane landed at Heathrow!

We laughed for the first time in ages on our New York trip with our dear friends and felt the short holiday had revitalised us. Pauline had unexpectedly lost her adored father when he was quite young and she, like me, had searched for mediums to give her the peace she needed. We talked about this a lot on our trip and it added to my belief that James was well and watching over me. Pauline had seen her father after he died as he appeared to her, whilst she was pregnant with her first child, every night. I longed to have that experience with James but, as Louise pointed out, it might make it worse as I would never want to let him go again.

Whilst lying in bed one night, I heard a noise downstairs as if someone was in the house. Then nothing. Silence: no footsteps up the stairs, no floorboards creaking. Total silence, and I thought it was just my imagination running on overtime. Lying motionless, I tried telling myself not to be so silly. I then heard the biggest sigh beside me on the bed. I realised it was a test for me to see if I would turn round and face whatever spirit was there, possibly James. However, I just could not turn round; I was too frightened. I realised on that night that actually seeing James would not be as easy as I once thought. Mediums are different, as they are used to seeing souls in spirit, but I was not. To say I was petrified would be understating my feelings. I knew it would be a long time, if ever, before I would see James appear to me in spirit. I was just not ready for it.

Out of all the nephews and nieces, my niece Emily was closest to James. Although Emily was younger, she loved the same things as James and it was Emily who James chose to visit in her dreams. We had already read that people who have passed make visits to their loved ones in the form of dreams so as not to scare them. Our minds are in a subconscious state when we are asleep so we are not alarmed.

In Emily's dream, she saw us all at my parents' house the Christmas after James had died. James appeared and asked how she was. She replied that she was fine and said she was shocked to see him. He said he was fine and then left as quickly as he had appeared. Emily was not shaken by this but was more worried about telling me in case it upset me; of course it didn't, and it gave me great comfort to know he was still watching over the family.

Sam was comforted on one occasion by a visit from James. She had gone to bed but found herself getting very cold. Having checked the heating thermostat, Sam discovered that it had somehow been turned to zero, and the front door was standing ajar as well. She closed the front door and went back to her bedroom, where she saw James standing there. Sam asked James to come in to bed for a cuddle but he said he couldn't stay long and pointed out that she had no clothes on. Sam said not to be silly, as she was his mum. James did what she asked, saying nothing. The cuddle seemed to last but really it was only moments. James then got up and spoke to her, saying that he had to go. She was begging him to stay and asked why, but all James would say was that he had to go.

Now this sounds like a vivid dream, but to Sam it was all so real at the time. Later on, speaking with Lisa Jayne, I learned that there is a way that spirits can communicate when you are just going off to sleep. We believe that James warned Sam that the front door was unlocked and did this by making her go downstairs to investigate the heating. As Sam had stated, she never turned the stat down so low that it was off. The next part – well, we shall have to make our own decisions on, but I feel that Sam was visited by James, only for a split moment, maybe in the hope that it would improve matters. We shall never know, but she was lucky to have had such a strong visit and James must have felt that it was needed.

TRAGEDY STRIKES AGAIN

We arrived back from New York at the beginning of March 2006. I had booked a trip to go to Dubai to see my customer there and was starting to get back into work. Whilst away, my sisters came to stay for a night with Louise and she was taking them to a local restaurant. Just before I left for Dubai, I suggested that Sam went along with them. She had started to go out with friends but always seemed to bump into James' friends and found it hard that he could not be with them. This ended up ruining her evening and she would flee home distraught.

Louise picked Sam up and they went back to our house for a quick drink before the taxi arrived to take them to the restaurant. Everything seemed fine. It was obvious to all of them that Sam was still in a lot of pain as she cried continuously throughout the meal but this was to be expected. By this time Sam and Mark had split up, the strain of losing James being too much for their relationship to survive and, without James there to keep the peace, things just did not seem to get better. Samantha no longer wanted to go to the places they had gone to with James, which I could understand, but she had grown to resent Mark for wanting to go to these places. I could also understand why he wanted to go there. As I have said before, everyone grieves in different ways so there is no right or wrong. It is said, when you lose a child, 75% of relationships don't survive afterwards. Louise and I were determined this was not going to happen to us, but then we were able to grieve together, on our own, in the only way we knew possible.

Sam said her days consisted of getting up, crying, taking another sleeping tablet and going back to bed. She was becoming a recluse, not even walking her dogs, and she got to the point where she could not visit James' grave any more. She would often wake in the early hours and look through the albums and letters of sympathy James' friends had written. None of this was healthy for her but everyone understood that this was her way of coping with the loss of James.

The evening came to an end and Sam went home whilst my sisters went back to our house with Louise. They talked about the evening and how they all felt Sam was not coping at all but felt there was nothing they could do to help as she had stopped answering calls and text messages. Sam cried constantly.

On visiting Sam one morning to see how she was, it was apparent all was not well. Like me, she was very low, which was only to be expected. As I arrived, we sat and had a coffee to talk about James and how we missed him so much. She said that the house was so quiet, and that she was waiting for the door to open and to hear a cry of "Mum!" James' room was on the ground floor of the town house where he had his own shower room and study. His routine was to come in, shout a greeting, and go straight into the shower – it was a routine that was never going to happen again and something Sam was finding very hard to get her head around. I glanced over to the corner of the kitchen and saw a number of shopping bags. I thought she had been out shopping, which surprised me, but almost reading my mind, she said, "Can you do me a favour and take these clothes back?" They were Christmas presents that James had chosen with Sam and she couldn't bear to have them around her, knowing he would never now get to wear them. Tears flowed down her face. I agreed, and took the bags away with me.

I did not really want to take the items back as I had only recently visited the shopping centre with James and it was going to be very hard for me, remembering him being there. However, I knew someone had to do it so I got in the car and headed for Bluewater Shopping Centre. Whilst driving, I was going over and over in my head what I was going to say. I was not comfortable with the usual excuse that 'we don't like it', as it was not the real reason for the returns. Sam had given me her credit card and pin number, as the refunds would only go back on that card. After parking up, I knew I was in for a difficult hour or so, openly explaining to strangers what had happened to my son.

Gathering the bags, I approached the entrance to the shopping centre, my heart pounding. Who was going to believe what I had to say as it sounded so far-fetched? How could it be true to a complete stranger who did not know me? I prayed that, after seeing my broken face the shop, assistants would believe me and not press for details. I went into the first shop and asked for the manager or manageress. I explained that I was there to return goods for a full refund after our terrible loss. All of the managers, without exception, were very sympathetic and refunded the card, dealing with the paperwork as best they could. No-one refused a refund, for which I was most grateful.

On walking out of the final shop, I could not help noticing the restaurant I had often visited with James, where we would laugh and talk about life in general. Now here I was, three weeks later, returning gifts that his mum had bought for him, and that he would never wear. The clothes would never be washed and never be screwed up on his bedroom floor. Distraught, I fled in tears.

Whenever I went round to see Sam, I tried to comfort her but often she felt that I was being too cold as I was not crying all the time. She had mentioned that her mum felt she should go into hospital to get some help but at the end of the day this was not Sam's choice. I just wanted her to grieve properly for James without tablets sedating her all the time, but looking back, I do not think Sam was strong enough to give up the tablets as they had helped her for three months. She sank more into her grief. Sam struggled to get out of bed and when she did, she stayed up for a while and then retreated back to the sanctuary of her bedroom.

Louise met Sam's mum, the night after the meal, at James' grave. She said Sam had called her when she got in and was in a total state, talking about ending her life. Of course, her mum went round there immediately to comfort her. She had started to take Sam's pills away and only give them to her when it was time to take them. Sam's mum really felt that she would try something silly. Louise listened but only truly knowing Sam since James' death, she felt there was nothing she could do. Sam had gone into herself and only really wanted to speak to anyone who was a blood relative of James, as she felt they were the only ones who truly felt as she felt. Sometimes I thought she did not want to come out of her grieving.

I came back from Dubai and, with a week to go to Mother's Day, I booked another appointment with Lisa. The date was set, 20th March. I had not spoken to Sam since being back.

The reading started and James came through straightaway. I explained to Lisa that I desperately wanted him to come to me so I could see him, but she explained that he would only do that when he felt I was ready. He confirmed the different things I had been up to for confirmation that he was around me. After half an hour or so, he suddenly went. Lisa couldn't believe it – she could not communicate with him any more. James just vanished from her mind. Puzzled, she told me he had gone. I just sat there; neither of us could understand it as he had come through so strongly. I just put it down to James wanting me to move on, almost as if he was saying he was not there at my beck and call but had to be allowed to get on with things himself. Lisa carried on with the reading. She told me she had an elderly lady with grey hair with her. Well, both my nans had grey hair and were elderly when they died. Lisa said it was the "one who you used to sing Edelweiss to." I was dumbfounded. Every Sunday as a boy, my dad's mum would come for dinner, and just before she left she would ask me to sit on her lap and sing Edelweiss to her.

After the reading, I went home as I did not want to go into work. Around 3.00 pm I had a call come up on my mobile – a number I did not recognise but I answered it anyway. It was a neighbour of Sam's I had met before and who had helped Sam a lot after James had died.

Sam was dead. She had taken her own life.

I couldn't believe it was happening all over again. Why had she done this? Sam could have spoken to me, to her mum, to her friends, but she always felt so alone, as if none of us knew what she was going through. Of course, it was always going to be harder for Sam as she had carried James for nine months but we all loved and missed him just the same. After splitting up with Mark, and without James around, Sam had sat for hours on end going over the events of 4th December, torturing her soul as to what had happened. Sam never really got any comfort in going to see a medium as she never really wanted to hear what they had to say; she just wanted James back, as we all did.

On 20th March, it seems Sam woke early, as a neighbour heard movement about 5.00 am. We knew she was looking through James' book of condolence as this was on the kitchen table. The dog walker had come in to take the dogs for a walk and called out to her. Sam was upstairs somewhere but she did answer back. Her mum had tried calling her but could not get an answer so she phoned the neighbour asking her to go over and check on Sam as the neighbour had a key. Sam's house was a three-storey town house, and upon entering, the neighbour said she knew something was not right. As she made her way up the stairs, she saw Sam's dead body.

The neighbour ran out into the street and called the police, who in turn told her not to touch the body as they needed to have forensics see it, but all the lady wanted to do was to make Sam comfortable. After three months of living without James, Sam obviously felt she could no longer live without him. She kept saying over and over again that she had nothing to live for, but she would not listen to reason. It was reported that Sam had no medication inside her. I can only imagine that she had had a moment of darkness and just flipped. I was devastated. The only living person able to truly know how I was feeling had just ended her life. The thought of James' mum taking her own life just broke me again. I could not imagine, even in my darkest days, taking my life, so I found it hard to think of others doing so. I truly believe though, that even if Sam had received help in those early days, she still would have taken her life. She was insistent that she had nothing to live for and life was not worth living.

I rushed over to the neighbour's house as the police were letting nobody into Sam's home. I phoned Louise and my father. Louise came straight over and my sisters were on their way down from London.

We all stood dumbfounded in the neighbour's kitchen. Mark was there, inconsolable. Even though he and Sam had separated, Mark still loved her but Sam felt as if she could not be around him as she slowly shut people out of her life. I really felt for Mark as many of Sam's friends blamed him for what had happened, but what can anyone do when someone asks them to leave and then refuses to take their call or answer the door?

Sam's two dogs were roaming around aimlessly. Mark offered to take these. He and I were allowed across to see Sam, by the police. I felt at that time she had a distressed look on her face, not at peace, and half of me wishes I had not seen her like this. I phoned Lisa as I now knew why James had left the reading earlier that day – he was going to welcome his mum. Lisa confirmed this and said she had both of them there. Sam was apologising for what she had done but had just wanted to be with James.

We left the neighbour's house and went to Sam's mum's house. She was in total disbelief and was just shaking, unable to believe what had happened. Her whole family had now been taken from her: James, her only grandson, and Sam, her only child. There was nothing we could say to her. Half of me was annoyed at Sam for what she had done. She had left her mum in such a state that she, too, now needed the doctor and now we had another funeral to arrange, so close to James'. I needed something to focus on and Carol, Sam's mum, asked me to arrange the funeral. She wanted it in West Malling church and for Sam to be buried near James' ashes. There was a plot right in front of James' that the vicar said we could have. I knew it was right as, when we went there, a white feather lay on the grass where Sam was to be laid to rest. We went the following day to lock Sam's house up, remove jewellery, turn off the heating, etc.

A month later when the house was emptied a note was found from Sam, which was passed on to me. Part of it read: "I am so sorry to leave you to grieve on your own, but I just could not bear to live without my baby boy. I miss him so much and want to be with him again. Thank you for all you have done for me. I will always love you."

The funeral was arranged. Louise had found a song by Evanescence, which really said how Sam had felt about losing James, so this was played. Carol had wanted Mark to stay away as tensions were running high but I did not think this was right. Instead he sat at the back of the church which, again, I did not agree with, but I wanted the day to go without any hassles. Our friends and family all came to the service and offered their support, and Louise had refreshed all of James' flowers on his grave so he looked smart for the day. The whole day went by so quickly as none of us could really believe we were there attending another funeral. Having James so close to the burial site made it feel as if we were burying his ashes all over again.

Once the day had passed, I tried to move on. I was the only one left to be strong for James, to make him proud, and I was determined to do just that. Louise and I booked a trip to Cyprus with our friends Mark and Kathy. Kathy was a great comfort as she had lost a lot of close people over her lifetime and was able to offer me words of advice and encouragement. I laughed with Mark as he made me forget everything but at the same time encouraged me to talk about James. They were both very fond of James and we reminisced, did stupid things, got merry and just did all we could to forget about our situation for a short time.

On the second night of the holiday we decided to eat out and found a quaint little restaurant in the town. We sat down listening to the background Cypriot music, as one does. We started to glance at the menus, when all of a sudden the James Blunt track 'Beautiful' came on. I was so pleased to hear it, but it was somewhat strange as it was played in a different context to the music we had been listening to whilst we settled down at the table. Kathy said, "There's your sign." I smiled and had a tear in my eye. As the track finished, the Cypriot music returned and played for the rest of the evening.

The holiday was exactly what I needed and I came back feeling ready to face work. I had taken on a new product and felt this was my way of getting back into the swing of things.

LEARNING TO LIVE

For Father's Day, Louise decided to get me a ticket to see Mia Dolan in action. She was holding a workshop in Thanet. We had tried and tried to get a reading with her through various people we knew but had hit a brick wall each time. Louise told me this was my only chance of speaking to her, and that if I could not arrange to get a reading on that day, then it was not meant to be.

I was so nervous going on my own as the whole day was a workshop designed to teach you how to read auras, the after-life and many things about reading people. I was worried I was going to be out of my depth. Everyone there was really nice and at the end Mia offered to do a book signing. I had taken the books Louise had bought and thought this my only chance. I approached the desk, sweating as I was so nervous she'd just brush me aside. I explained how I had tried to get a reading through friends of friends – but to no avail. She was extremely kind and said how sorry she was but she only read people who had lost children or worse. I explained that my situation was worse. Intrigued, she paused, leant forward and told me how I could get hold of her. I was on cloud nine coming out of the theatre. I immediately called Louise who was thrilled for me. It may sound strange but when you have lost a child or someone close and you know there is someone out there who can help you or assist you in your grief, you cling to that. Mia had now given me hope and I knew she was going to be just what I needed. I felt it was fate that she was from the same place as Louise – that's the reason we had bought her books in the first place. She, too, had lost a son roughly the same age as James.

The following week at work, I stressed and stressed about calling Mia, worried that she would not remember me or that she had changed her mind. In the end, Louise just shouted at me to "Bloody call her!" I called, and we made the date for the following week to have the reading. Mia explained that, as James had passed recently, then she would not get anything from him but, to both our amazements on the day, he came through. She told me the usual: how I had arrived in a big, black car (even though I had parked two streets away), and she described Louise and me to a tee. Mia then went on to Sam and how she had passed. She described my business and business associates whom I had only just met. It was astounding.

I had prepared a number of questions to ask her, as I now believed in reincarnation I was worried that James might reincarnate before I died and I would never get to see him again. She explained that this could not happen as there always had to be three generations of one family in heaven at any one time and that, when it was my turn to pass over, James would be there waiting for me. I loved her openness and her honesty and I felt completely at ease with her. She spoke about her own grief and how she thought I was strong in my grief, visiting James each week and talking so openly about him.

All in all, by having this reading with Mia, as with the readings I had had in the past, I came away with less weight on my shoulders as each time James did not fail to come through, reconfirming my thoughts that he was with me all the time.

Time passed and Louise and I were still trying to live as best we could in the circumstances, readjusting to life as it had become. There was always something to knock me back a few paces though. Sam's mum had asked not to be told how Sam had died. This I could understand, as she felt knowing the cause of Sam's death would make it harder for her to come to terms with it. Obviously, as I had shared custody of James, when he died his main residence was listed as Bearsted, on his provisional licence and other documents.

About three months after Sam had died, the local village newspaper decided to write a piece on Sam's inquest, justifying it on the basis that James had lived in Bearsted. The article made Sam sound like a mad woman who drove around all day passing her son's school, watching the children come out, when in fact James had already left the school and moved on to college. We were livid and Louise wrote a letter to the editor voicing her disgust at what he had written, and stating that if he really wanted to know what had happened, he should have contacted one of us rather than exaggerating a story that was incorrect. Of course, as with any newspaper that cannot find enough stories to write about, the reply was unapologetic, unsympathetic and even stated how they would be reporting on the trial that was due to start shortly.

Shortly after this, we were sitting one Saturday watching television when I happened to flick through the local area paper and saw an article about Sam and James. I could not believe what I was reading. In his wisdom, Carol's husband, Ray, had gone to the local paper to place something in it and happened to 'bump' into the editor who asked about James and Sam. He went on to make out that Sam was a single parent who brought James up on her own and that he was the grandfather that James had never had. I was livid. Anyone who did not know me would think I was no part of James' life. I was also upset that Carol's husband could write something like this that was just so untrue. Sam and I shared custody of James 50/50. I was the one who provided for his schooling; a house for him to live in with the lifestyle he was used to, unconditional love; his pocket money; his whole support. I could not have been more of a hands-on father to James if we had lived together 24/7. Now he was gone I had someone, who knew James only for the later part of his life, making out that I was no part of James' life and that he was raised entirely by his mum. We texted Carol the next day to stress how upset we were and she made Ray go back to the editor and print an apology. However, of course you know yourself, once you read an untrue story in the papers the apology is a small section of a large page which no-one bothers to read in the next issue!

I continued my contact with Lisa and after a few weeks I felt I wanted to go and see her again. They say you know when you should go and I had got to that stage again. I needed another confirmation that James was OK, that he was still around me and that one day I would see him again. I reiterated to Lisa this was my main reason for going, and to my amazement she asked if I wanted to see James. I did not really understand what she was asking. Did she want me to see him dead? She said she felt I was ready, and as I was desperate to have the smallest contact with James, I immediately agreed.

Lisa meditated for a while and showed me how to meditate, which relaxed me. She then started telling me what I can only describe as a story. In my mind we were walking through the woods, passing tree after tree on rough ground until we came to an empty tree trunk. She asked me to describe the tree trunk to her, which I did – it was hollow, or so it seemed as I looked down on it. Lisa told me in my mind to bend down and look into the tree trunk where I would see a mirror. In my mind I bent down and saw the mirror. Upon closer inspection, it was not my reflection that was staring back at me but James'. I was slightly taken aback as I did not expect to see him. It was simply for a split second but it was long enough for me to come out of that reading knowing I had been able to move on that little bit further.

Weeks went by, and as they did, people noticed that I was getting stronger. I was able to go out to visit friends although I never felt quite ready to go out socially. Louise and I were invited out but I always managed to get out of it which sounds quite harsh, especially as our friends are wonderful, but I just didn't feel ready.

Eventually we were invited out and I said I would go – just for a meal with friends at a local restaurant. On the actual day, I was feeling quite down thinking of James and did not want to go. As a passing gesture, I said to Louise that she should still go, thinking she would say, "No, I'll stay with you," as she had done over the last few months, but she said, "OK, if you are sure!!" She said afterwards that she had to be cruel to be kind. Louise knew I could go on forever making excuses and that it would be no good for me in the long term. She also knew that I would hate being home alone, a fact which became obvious as I kept texting her all evening, but it worked, and again something so small made me a little bit stronger and able to start going out again.

We still had no word from the police as to how their investigations were going until one Saturday when Graham, our Family Liaison Officer, phoned to say he had just heard that the Crown Prosecution Service had decided to bring charges of 'Death by dangerous driving' on the boy who had been in charge of the car on the night James was killed. We were so pleased that it finally looked as if James would get justice and we could start to move further forward.

That summer Louise and I booked a holiday to the Maldives – we wanted to go somewhere we had never been before and somewhere where we could just relax and read, swim and generally be by ourselves. We had the most amazing time there: we sat and read, the staff were so friendly and welcoming, and we had the most memorable time. Every night as we passed the bar a song would come on, 'Tears in Heaven', 'Knocking on Heaven's Door', 'You're Beautiful' – all of these being a great comfort to me and more signs, I felt, from James.

Sam and James' house eventually sold later in the year to a couple with a young baby whom I felt were the ideal choice to bring some life back into the house. I busied myself with work, visiting customers and generally keeping my mind occupied, even though James was on my mind all day long from the time I woke up to the time I went to bed. I even dreamed about him sometimes but he never appeared the same as he was when he died. I am told this is totally normal but I still wished for the day that I might see him. You hear about people seeing their dead loved ones and I desperately wanted one more time with James but, as Louise reminded me, one more time would never be enough and I would continue wanting to see him more and more.

James' last school, Sackville, asked if they could plant a tree in his memory, which I thought was a wonderful idea, and they did a planting ceremony which we attended. So James' memory will live on and on at the school for years to come. The headmistress was fond of James and she made every effort to ensure the planting went smoothly. We sat in her office and joked that the last time we were there was probably because James had been in some bother, nothing too serious but just playing the jester and getting into trouble with some teachers.

Kathy and Mark had won an auction to name a small boat at their local marina and they named it 'Beautiful Boy' in James' memory. He would have loved that as he loved boating and being on the water.

The day I dreaded was Father's Day. Every shop you go into nowadays has Father's Day memorabilia and there was no hiding from it. I was still a father and if people asked me if I had children I always said yes, but James was not here to see me on Father's Day. That Sunday morning Louise came downstairs with a card and a gift. She had the same opinion as me: I was still a father so deserved a Father's Day card and gift. Her gift was a trip to see John Edward, the famous American medium based near New York who I thought was unbelievable when I saw him on the TV. I couldn't believe it. It was a wonderful gift. I was going to fly out to New Jersey, stay in a hotel near to the theatre where the meeting was taking place, have a day or two to myself and then fly back. Luckily, a long-time friend of mine, unbeknown to Louise, lived quite close by so I arranged to meet up with him and his wife.

I flew out to New York on a Friday, picked up my tickets for the show the next evening and settled down for an evening with Mike and Kelly, reminiscing about old times. On the day itself I was quite nervous. I have learned that this is the natural way to be, as 99% of the people going to such evenings are hoping and praying to get a message from a lost loved one. I was no different. It is at shows like this that you realise you are not alone in your grieving. The number of people there that had lost children was overwhelming. Of course, some of them had died in horrible circumstances.

I did not get a reading that night but I did learn a valuable lesson – whatever problem one might have, there are always people somewhere in the world who are in a much worse position. However terrible losing a child is, at least I could identify James, I could kiss his warm head goodbye, I could stroke his hair and give him a proper funeral. Some people never have this chance. Some people can never identify the child they have lost. Some people never have a body to bury or cremate or a forehead to kiss. In a strange way I considered myself lucky amongst the people in that room. I came away from New York with a more positive frame of mind and was determined that no-one was going to pull me down.

Whilst I was in New York, Louise had arranged to have a tree planted at our local park in memory of James. It was a wonderful surprise on my return and each year it has produced beautiful pink cherry blossom.

We had sold our boat as James spent so much time on it I just wanted rid of it, so in the summer we now had a great deal of spare time. We used to go to my parents of a Sunday for lunch. The nieces and nephews would come over and play in the pool but my dad just could not bring himself to join in the fun. He sat in the lounge on his own as he could not bear to see the youngsters all playing without James joining in the fun. James was always the big cousin and the others idolised him. We could see that the smaller kids could not understand why Grandad did not come out with everyone but it was too difficult to explain to them. We could not mention James' name without my dad getting upset. He just could not talk about what had happened or even talk about the wonderful times we had had with James. It helped me to talk to anyone who would listen but, as I have said before, everyone grieves in different ways. There is no right or wrong way; you just have to get through it in as best a way you can.

The year seemed to go quite quickly as we purposely tried to keep ourselves busy, giving ourselves things to focus on. The anniversary of James' death was upon us in a flash. We arranged for fresh flower arrangements to be done. I took fresh flowers up to the grave every Friday morning but special posies were done for 4th December. My parents and Debbie, my sister, came down to lay flowers and we spent a quiet day by ourselves. With all days that you dread so much, this was not as bad as I thought it was going to be. It was a peaceful and reflective day and we talked about James as much as we could. My dad was still getting upset but was now not as bad as previous times. He was able to reminisce about James in a way he never could before. In the evening, James' friends invited us to their local pub to have a drink in his honour. We went but only stayed a while. It was lovely seeing them all and knowing that his friends will never forget James.

Just before Christmas the headmaster at Radlett Prep called to say they would like to plant a tree in James' honour. My nieces, Emily and Katie, were still at the school so they would be responsible for looking after the tree. They met us at the school along with my parents. My dad arrived all flushed but for no reason that we could think of. He was not late. Dad said he had been driving along, getting warmer and warmer, when he looked down and noticed the heated seats were on – something he had never activated. Remembering the trip to France with Louise's dad, I knew this was James and he was using his warped sense of humour letting us know he was there.

Christmas Day that year was spent at my parents'. Louise had bought me a karaoke system and we spent the whole of Christmas on it, passing the time away. This carried on at our house on Boxing Day. This Christmas I decided to treat my sisters to a trip to New York with Louise and me and we flew out after the Boat Show, in the middle of January. They had never been to New York before and the girls shopped and shopped and shopped, and we all laughed and had a great time. It really helped to keep our minds occupied as the trial of the car driver was due to start on 24th January, a week after we arrived home.

THE TRIAL

The trial was scheduled to be heard in Maidstone Crown Court for four days, possibly five if the jury could not make a decision. We were all nervous. We were worried that James' death would be in vain and I was not looking forward to seeing the boy who was responsible for his death. My sister Debbie came down for the trial for support; Louise and I were of course there, my friend John who was also James' godfather, Carol and Ray and one of Sam's friends were all sat in the public gallery. Most of us had never been in a courtroom before, especially under these circumstances, and it was quite daunting to see it.

Before the trial started, we met with Graham, our Police Liaison Officer who was to be there throughout the whole trial, the police who handled the investigation, and the barrister acting for the CPS (Crown Prosecution Service). The Police Liaison Officer explained that it was highly likely the trial would never reach the end as it would probably be thrown out due to technicalities. My heart sunk. This was a year and a month after James had died and it seemed it would never end. Now it looked like we would not get any justice for James.

Day One was to see evidence from the father and son in the oncoming vehicle and the father and son in the vehicle behind them, as they were all travelling in convoy to a football match. Even though these boys were only about 16 years old at the time, the mature way they delivered their evidence impressed all of us.

It was unbearable as we sat whilst the jury flicked through photos of the accident. I couldn't look. There were photos of the mangled car in various positions; photos of the site where the accident happened, and photos of the approach to the accident site. The father in the oncoming vehicle described how, as he came round the corner, the Corsa in which James was a passenger seemed to be zig-zagging across the carriageway until suddenly it seemed to lose control and came straight across his path. He hit the passenger side where James was sitting. The car went up in the air, mounted a foot-high grass verge and continued travelling before coming to rest by hitting a ragstone wall. The guy said he was doing about 50 mph but the Corsa appeared to be going much faster. This poor man had been off work for months, due to stress. I really felt for him. He, like me, was obviously a really caring father who had bothered making the effort by taking his son to a football match. In fact, I think he may even have been the coach, I can't remember. The boys described a similar view of the car coming round the corner.

That first day was quite a strain. The prosecuting barrister who, rightly so, was doing his job, questioned the young men in a manner I was uncomfortable with. He made them sound as if they had seen something totally different, but they stuck to their version of what they had seen. The prosecuting barrister asked if the car had merely swerved into their path, but the witnesses were adamant that the car was definitely zig-zagging as they came around the corner.

We left the court after the first day and I came home and fell asleep; I was so emotionally drained. It was very hard to sit in court and hear all about the impact of the oncoming car and what that impact would have done to James, knowing he was sitting in the passenger seat.

The following day the court heard the evidence of the investigating officers. They were incredible. Even the judge commented at the end how precise their evidence was. The investigating officers described, according to the evidence, what had happened. They were able to measure the skid mark on the road to determine that the car was travelling at least 75 mph in a 60 mph speed limit. The car had hit no curb to make it career across the road so we can only surmise, from the eye-witness accounts, that the driver was simply showing off and snaking the car in the road before losing control due to the speed at which it was travelling. Again, the police were cross-examined, but being used to their day in court, they seemed as cool as anything under pressure. We were warned by our barrister that the defence barrister could still ask for the trial to be thrown out, but we went the whole of Tuesday with no such request being made.

Again, I came home and slept. The next day we would hear evidence from the driver: a day Louise always felt sure would convince the jury of his guilt. The evidence had proved the driver was speeding, even though he said he was not. It was just up to the jury now to make their minds up.

That night Emily had another dream: a visit from James. Emily described a scene that happened the previous year where we were all in my parents' kitchen. James was also there for a split second and asked her to tell his dad that everything would be OK, to be patient, and not to worry.

We sat in the courtroom on the Wednesday morning, having been told that this was the last day the trial could come to a halt if requested. The driver's time in the witness box came. He walked past us, head down. He mumbled whilst in the witness box and rarely looked up. The driver told how he had called for James around lunchtime, to go into Maidstone as James wanted to get his mum her presents for Christmas. Straightaway I knew this to be a lie as every year James and I would go out and get his mum's presents and vice versa. I had already taken James out the previous week to get all of the presents on Sam's list. They were in fact going into Maidstone to get a McDonald's, but getting parents' Christmas presents, I suppose, sounded better for a jury.

The car took the A26 into Maidstone and the boys were apparently talking and listening to music. The driver said that something small, possibly a cat or a fox, had run out in front of the car. The CPS barrister asked the driver to point to the spot where he was when the said animal ran out. He pointed to an area which had no bushes at the side of the road, about 50m from the accident site. The barrister sounded amazed as he asked how the driver could not have seen the animal in the distance in such an open space, especially as he still insisted he was doing around 50 mph. It was suggested that the driver had had enough time to apply the brakes if this was the spot where the animal ran out.

The judge asked the driver to show how far he was away from the animal before seeing it. He indicated a measurement of about 1-1½ metres, to which the judge announced her surprise at how he could see anything at that distance when he was proven to be doing at least 75 mph. We hoped this had convinced the jury, but had no way of knowing.

During the driver's evidence, we had to leave the room at certain times as it was too much to bear. As the CPS barrister cross-examined him and his evidence was pulled to pieces, we felt more confident at the end of the day that some form of justice would be seen. From this moment on we knew there was no going back as there was no way they could ask for a mis-trial.

Returning home that night, my doubts returned and I was convinced the driver was going to walk away. Louise just kept telling me to have faith: faith in the legal system and faith in myself that it would all come right.

The summing-up on Thursday by the defence barrister told the jury how the driver had got engaged at Christmas and was looking to settle down with his girlfriend. This was so upsetting as it just went to prove how he had continued with his life whilst James' had been taken in such tragic circumstances. We honestly believe the judge saw this too. The court heard how the driver was an apprentice, halfway through his apprenticeship. Luckily for his family, he was able to get a job as James never got that far. Of course, the summing-up from each side always sounded as if it was going to go with whichever barrister was speaking at the time. The jury were then dismissed to reach a verdict and we were told to go off for lunch.

I did not want to be with anyone – I just wanted to walk around trying to get my head around what might happen. I left everyone to go to a local cafe. As Louise and Debbie walked into the cafe the

Take That song, 'Have a Little Patience' was playing and they took that as a sign from James, especially following Emily's dream. As I walked around Maidstone, totally unaware of what was going on in the cafe, the same Take That song came into my head and would not leave! I walked and walked, trying to put the whole thing out of my mind but never being able to escape the possibility that the driver could get off.

We met back in the waiting area of the courtroom at about 2.00 pm. The CPS barrister came out and said that the judge had called them into her chambers to discuss whether the Victim Impact Statement, something that I had to prepare for the court, would be read out. The barrister took this as a sign that the judge was expecting a guilty verdict as this is the only time the statement can be read, but we did not want to get our hopes up. The Impact Statement is something that the victim's family can prepare, to highlight to the court how the crime has affected them and how their lives have changed. It is a way of giving them a voice in the whole procedure.

We were so nervous outside the court that I broke down – the emotions of the week just became too much. I so wanted James to get justice of some kind but it was out of our hands. There was nothing we could do to help the situation. The evidence had to speak for itself.

We were called back into the courtroom at 3.00 pm. Hearts pounding, we sat as the jury entered, followed by the judge. She asked the foreman to stand and she read out the charge. She asked the foreman to give the verdict of the jury. Our hearts were in our mouths – the whole week had built up to this one moment. I was shaking, holding Louise's hand and praying it had not all been in vain.

The foreman read the verdict of the jury... Guilty. We all burst into tears, tears of relief, tears of joy that the driver would have to face some form of punishment for his actions. We sobbed and hugged and sobbed and smiled. Emotions, not just from that week but from the day of James' passing, came out. We had finally got justice for James after more than a year of waiting.

The judge told the jury they could leave if they wanted, or they could remain to hear the Impact Statement as the court was drawing to a close. About half of the jury stayed. They stayed to hear the judge tell everyone that the driver had only passed his test ten days before the accident and that he had no insurance.

The CPS barrister then read out my Impact Statement. I looked over at the remaining members of the jury and they were in tears. Tears at learning what had happened to us as a family and tears of relief, I think, that they had given the correct verdict based solely on the evidence in the courtroom.

This is my statement:

IMPACT STATEMENT – MICHAEL BOLLOM

Family life as I knew it ended dramatically on the 4th December 2005 when my beloved son James was killed in a car accident.

I received a call from James' distraught mum at approximately 4.15 pm – a call which I know will haunt me for the rest of my life.

I was the only one strong enough to go to the hospital to identify James. Part of me kept thinking it was all a terrible mistake and that when I reached the hospital it would turn out to be someone else. I had tried to get hold of James all afternoon on his mobile phone. Before that day, when I called if James was in a bad signal area, he would call back within five minutes. Not receiving the call gave me butterflies.

I identified James and visited his mother's house before returning home to face my distraught family. My father was in pieces and we were all in a state of shock. This never happens to people like us, it is only something you hear on the news about other people. How wrong we were…

Making funeral arrangements for James was the longest week of our lives, something we never, ever imagined we would have to do. To have to pick out wording for the order of service, the music, the flowers, all became too much. To add to our grief, we had to cope with the dark hole James' personality had left. We all missed him so much, even silly little things like hearing my phone ring – whenever it rang, nine times out of ten it would be James ringing to fill me in on his day, what he had been up to, what he was getting up to, his plans for the weekend.

To try to come to terms with what had happened, we visited the crash site the following day. Later in the week, the police called, advising us that they had to stop the traffic along the A26 as approximately 120 friends of James from Kings Hill all walked up to the crash site to lay flowers and candles and the police were worried about their safety. They left flowers, cards, photographs, cuddly toys, even a can of Coke as this was his preferred drink. We gained some comfort knowing James was so well liked, but we knew our lives would never be the same again. Having to phone around friends and family and tell them what had happened was torture, especially as this time of year was Christmas. The response from everyone was the same: "Not James! Please tell us it's not James?"

James was my only child and was idolised not just by myself but by all the members of his family, from his grandparents to his smaller cousins who referred to him as Big James. He mixed with any walk of life, any age, and was popular not only in school but everywhere he went.

James was a very popular boy, more popular than we ever realised when over 400 people turned up at his funeral on Friday 9th December. We pulled up at the crematorium to a mass of cars and faces. Most had to stand out in the cold as there was not enough room inside the Chapel of Rest.

The last school James attended, Sackville, brought children in their minibuses to pay their respects. James' primary school teachers were there, whom he had not seen for a number of years but all remembered him with such affection; his college teachers were there, as he had just started a Business Studies course. Everyone loved James for his sense of humour, his politeness and most of all, his smile. I felt and still feel proud to have raised such a son.

The ceremony was unbearable. Never did I think I would have to attend a service where I would be laying my son to rest.

We played James Blunt's 'Beautiful' at the funeral, as this was a favourite song of James and I am told that this had to be played five times to allow people to filter through the crematorium chapel. The song was such a fitting one as 'Beautiful' described James – inside and out.

Christmas came and went. I received an album of James' photos for Christmas, photos that covered his school days, his hobbies, our holidays together, opening his presents on Christmas Day – every pose imaginable. I look back at this album all the time, remembering the times we shared together, times I will never forget.

On New Year's Eve my wife and I went for an early meal with James' mum and her partner as none of us wanted to be awake for the dreaded 12 o'clock. We found some comfort with each other swapping stories of James but found it heart-breaking not having him there and knowing he would not return home to tell us about his evening.

James' 17th Birthday was on 9th January 2006. We visited his grave and laid fresh flowers, as did most of the family and his friends. Knowing he would have been taking his first driving lesson on this day made it all the more hard to bear.

James' mum found it equally as hard coming to terms with James not being here any more. Living round the corner from the driver did not help her situation and she asked on a number of times for him to contact her, just to find out what happened. She did not want to be judge or jury but wanted, in her own mind, to know what James had been talking about or whether he was happy when the accident occurred. She never received any reply and it tortured her, feeling as if the driver's life had not changed when James' life had ended. I felt the same way. James' mum, Samantha, asked that the driver's family have the courtesy even just to pull their curtains of an evening so she would not have to see them sitting around as a family, but again, nothing. The only feedback Samantha received was a complaint made by the family to the police that she was harassing them. How two heartfelt letters were harassment, considering what we had been through, I do not know.

Samantha was told by some friends that they had seen the driver go straight to the Spitfire pub in Kings Hill upon his release from hospital. He did not have the common sense or the decency to respect our grief and keep a low profile. This attitude was also demonstrated when my wife and I went to a restaurant in Maidstone with friends. The driver was also in the restaurant, although I did not see him. However, my wife did, and she was seen by him yet, after a short period, he continued partying with his friends. It did not seem to us that the driver realised how his actions had ruined the lives of James' family and friends.

March 20th was another tragedy in my life. A tragedy which only happened because James was taken from us. Samantha, James' mum, took her life as she felt she had nothing to live for once James had gone. The memories of him in the house used to haunt her and she could find no comfort from anyone or anything. She had the memories, constantly, of all his friends living in such close proximity and she could not bear the thought that James was not with them. Receiving no answers to her questions from the driver's family made it worse.

Samantha was the one person who knew exactly what I was going through and was the one person who had raised James with me since birth. Even though we were divorced, James had always been our Number One priority and because of this he grew up into a very well adjusted boy who seemed to be fazed by nothing, who would help anyone and never had a bad word to say about anything.

James was a boy who would always kiss me in front of his friends as we had an immensely close bond. I would take him shopping to Bluewater, another place which is unbearable as seeing the groups of young boys there just reminds me of him. James would come out with us when we went to dinner with friends, if he was not doing anything himself, and all of our friends treated him as an equal as he had the ability to talk to anyone whether it be a boy his own age, a toddler or an O.A.P. He was never rude and I never had any trouble with him being a typical moody teenager as he just was not that kind of boy.

James would often come into work with me during the school holidays. After the accident I felt I would never go back to work again but gradually I have returned, often leaving early. I still feel that I am working for nothing as, now James has gone, there is no-one for me to leave anything to or to work that extra bit harder for. To make matters worse, we had even set up a desk at the office especially for James when he came into work. This desk is still there and is still considered to be James' desk.

James' favourite food was Chinese; he could have eaten it every night had he been allowed. We have been unable to return to his favourite Chinese restaurant since as we always sat in the same place and had the same meal. Again, the owners of the Chinese always asked after James if he was not with us.

James regularly came to the cinema with us. He was never embarrassed to sit with us as some young teenagers are. Again, I feel I cannot go to the cinema yet, as each time I think of James raving about the latest film. Even simple things such as going out for dinner is now so hard as I often see teenagers wearing the same fashions that James did, having their hair cut the same way, chatting on their mobile phones – all things that were part and parcel of James' everyday life.

James and I would speak up to four times a day whether he was staying at our house or with his mum in Kings Hill. Now my phone rarely rings. We would always end the call with "Love you". Love sums up the relationship James and I had as father and son. We had an unbreakable bond and were extremely close. It is this closeness that I miss so much.

James was cremated and his ashes were buried at West Malling church. We chose this church not only because it is peaceful but because it is near to his friends' schools and they can come and visit him. Many times I have been there and some of his friends have come along to see him. Valentine's Day saw an abundance of flowers left by James' many female admirers as well as his friends. I now take every Friday off from work to visit

James' grave to try to get comfort. He always has an immaculate grave as he was always immaculate in life.

Family and friends made donations in the weeks following James' death and with this money we bought two benches in James' memory: one now stands on the Green in Bearsted overlooking the fish pond as James was an avid fisherman; the other is on Kings Hill. I often go and sit on the bench in Bearsted and reflect on my loss, remember James as a young child running around the village fete, going to dinner at the restaurants on the village green and seeing James run to the bakery every Saturday to pick up the cakes they had reserved for him knowing they were popular and could sell out.

His primary school in London have planted a tree in James' memory as he was so well liked there, whilst his senior school are naming a fishing competition after him as he would go every year with the school for a week's fishing. They also had a tree-planting ceremony in November in memory of James. The whole school came along and all of his family and friends each placed soil over the roots of the tree so we could all feel as if we had planted it for James. His headmistress commented that even her school life is not the same now that James is no longer there.

Knowing I will never, in this lifetime, talk to my son again, cuddle him, kiss him, run him around, treat him to different things, talk about his future with him and just do the normal things that we did together, is something that I have to live with for the rest of my life. In a matter of seconds, this was taken from me and my life sentence began.

I have had to accept that my life will never be the same again. Unfortunately, there is nothing I can do to change this and I know I will never get over what has happened.

There is not a minute in the day that goes by when I do not think of James. Everywhere I look in the house, he is there and this is the way I prefer it. We talk about him every day, looking back on the fond memories we have but knowing now that these are just memories.

We are not a family that are looking for revenge; however, we are a family that are looking for justice. Justice for James who was taken from us at such an early stage and justice for our family who all have had to look at their lives and try and live them the best they can. We would like the guilty party in this to realise what impact losing James has had on our family as well as his friends, many of whom were given counselling to deal with their loss. I know nothing will ever bring James back to me but I would like to know what his last thoughts were and what was discussed in the car. Was he happy in his last few moments? I really feel this is not a lot to ask, as I have lost everything, but I could gain some comfort if I knew the details of James' last moments of life.

The courtroom sat in silence listening to the Impact Statement and we muffled tears throughout the whole statement, remembering just what we had lost.

The judge announced that sentencing would be in March and the driver's barrister asked for bail. The judge refused and ordered him down to the cells immediately. We could not believe it. We never expected that and I am sure neither did he, but we didn't care about the driver. He had taken the most precious thing from our lives. Of course, we accept it was an accident, but people have to take the consequences for their actions. The evidence proved the driver was lying about his speed. It suggested that he was lying about swerving to avoid some sort of animal and he never once said sorry for his actions. The driver never showed any remorse in the witness box as he kept insisting he was not speeding. We just wanted the truth in that courtroom, but when that day came, we knew we were never going to get it. How could we get the truth when the driver himself wouldn't admit it? We wanted to know if James was laughing in the car, what they were talking about, and whether he was being jovial. We wanted any minute details of James' last minutes, just to try and make the situation slightly easier to accept. But we have received none of these details. If the driver had sat in the witness box and expressed his sorrow, maybe it would have made us feel slightly better, but he never has. There has been no anguish, no grief, no remorse.

The sentencing was set for March. Just over six weeks to wait to close this chapter of our lives and to get on with living them as best we could. I wasn't going to go to the sentencing; however, Louise wanted to go to see it through. Graham, our Family Liaison Officer, had arranged to pick her up and at the last minute I decided I should also go. The sentencing took place in Canterbury as this is where the judge usually resides. We had a different barrister allocated to the case by the CPS and he talked us through what would happen. The driver's father got up to make a plea to the court. He said his son was only young, had his whole life ahead of him and that he, as a father, could never comprehend what we had been through and we believed him to be genuine. However, I couldn't help feeling that even though his son was only young, he was old enough to drive and to face the responsibilities that this brings, both to passengers in the car and to other drivers on the road. The driver's father assumed the driver was covered by his own car insurance, as he was fully comprehensive, but this was found not to be the case.

The judge then gave the probationer's report and the probationer highlighted that, in her opinion, the driver still showed no remorse for the accident. His solicitor made the usual pleas and sentencing was passed at two years. We all knew the driver would probably only serve half his time, but a week in a young offender institute is more than we would ever want to stay so a year would be enough time for him to reflect on what had happened.

Graham drove us back home, and as we sat in the police car, we both knew James would be sitting there egging us to press one of the buttons to turn the lights on or the sirens; in fact, he would have been driving Graham mad getting him to press everything. This thought brought some light relief after such a dreadful day.

After sentencing was passed we were contacted by a Victim Support Worker, Sharon. She was put in place to liaise with us, advising us of when the release date would be set, how we felt as victims, how the release would impact us, etc. We got on great with Sharon and felt like she really was on our side and looking out for us. She explained that, of course, the driver would not serve the full sentence and that the release date would not be around any sensitive dates such as James' birthday, the anniversary of his death or Christmas.

We never imagined we would get a call four months later to say the driver could be released at any time. We were devastated. The whole court case seemed to have been a shambles. What was the point of awarding a sentence of two years and then releasing him after four months? We were interviewed by Sharon and explained how upset we were that this could happen. Sharon relayed our viewpoint in her report and it was decided, by the Prison Governor, that the driver would serve the whole year. I do not want to spend too much time considering the sentencing, but anyone who has lost someone so close to them, in such circumstances, wants justice and it all felt such a sham.

MY BELIEFS

Before James passed over, I remember flicking through the TV channels and coming across various shows featuring mediums. 'What a load of rubbish,' I thought. How could these people know these things? They must plant people in the audience, or in the queues waiting to go inside, and find out information. It was all hyped up for TV. Now my beliefs have swung round 360 degrees and I totally believe in the power of the spirit world. I believe spirits have the power to communicate through mediums, that they have the power to give signs to the living, and that they have the power to come to us through our dreams. When you lose someone so young and so close to you, you reach out looking for answers. I have always been inquisitive; that's my nature. Not knowing something makes me look into it further and this is exactly what I did after James' passing. We read and read books on spirits, angels, mediums, life after death, and every single one had the same message: We don't die. Our bodies die but our souls live on.

Have you ever met someone you get on so well with you that you feel as if you have known them before? You probably have. Our friends and close family in life are usually part of our soul group. In another life I may have been James' brother. Who knows? But I know with all my heart that I will see James again and be part of his soul group in heaven. I was recommended to watch the film of a book written by Mitch Albom, 'The Five People You Meet on the Way to Heaven,' starring Jon Voight. It is a story of a man who goes through life making mistakes, correcting them and then making more. He dies and the film shows his journey to heaven, whilst going back over his mistakes and how everyone he met in his life on the way to heaven had taught him a new lesson.

I often get asked if I believe in God, especially knowing that He could take someone away from me in such tragic circumstances – but the answer is yes, I believe in God. I believe that whatever James was doing on that fateful day he would have died, as that was his time. Whether he was walking across the road, plugging some electrical device in, whatever, James would have died on 4th December. We all go through life learning lessons. Bad things are thrown at us and we learn from them. My lesson from James' passing was that material things do not matter any more. Yes, I like nice things, but I look at things differently now. I am not afraid of dying as I know James will be waiting for me. I am more compassionate when other people suffer a misfortune and at the end of the day I know that, whatever I have gone through in life, there are always people out there who have suffered much worse than me.

I attend medium shows, such as those featuring John Edward and Gordon Smith. Once, at an evening with Gordon Smith in London, he had a young boy come through with spiky hair. About 50 people put their hands up to acknowledge the reading could be for them. Gordon continued… "A 16-17 year old." Ten people dropped their hands… "A bench has been dedicated to his memory…" Five people dropped their hands… "This person died in a car crash. He had a CD made of his favourite songs…" All of this could have been for me and there were still 20 or so people with their hands up. What lesson did I learn from this? That I am not alone. There are hundreds, thousands, of families out there who have lost people in the way I lost James. Having to cope with the aftermath of James' death did not make me special in any way, although dying at such a young age made James special as he achieved so much in his lifetime.

Why did James never come through at public medium events? Because I did not need him to. There were distraught people at these events who had lost loved ones, who were never able to get the comfort that I got through Lisa Jayne and Mia Dolan. I believe James is with me all of the time, looking after me, watching my back, guiding me on the right path. After Sam's funeral, my mother was in the house alone one Sunday morning. My mother's Alzheimer's disease was gradually getting worse but at this time she was still able to understand what was going on around her. She walked out of her kitchen towards the hallway and something made her look back, but why? It's not something she would ever be likely to do as she had no reason to. As she looked back, my mother could see her kitchen ceiling was on fire. A transformer in the lights had ignited the dried flowers she had in the kitchen and the ceiling was full of flames. She called my sister, in the confusion saying she was on fire. Of course, my sister realised my mother herself was not on fire and quickly called a neighbour who went round and managed to extinguish the flames. Why had Mum turned around? If she had carried on, the whole house would have burned down but something in her head made her turn around. Someone was telling her to look back, and thank God she did.

I often feel James around me and it's always at a time when I feel low. I can almost feel him move in closer as if to engulf me with a big cuddle and it makes me feel so much better. I often travel with my work and I feel James then, wherever it is in the world. I had to travel to Australia to see a customer after the trial. My customer, Jimmy, said his wife was a trained medium but she never told anyone; even family members did not know she had the gift. As soon as I arrived, she told me she had to give me a reading. It was more like James was telling Jimmy's wife to take me aside whilst he confirmed things through her about what I was up to, where my business was going, everything. I had only just met Theresa and she gave me the reading of my life. She told me my Uncle Jack was talking to her and that he was surrounded by paint. He had a paint manufacturing business. Theresa told me how James had a blue teddy with him. This teddy I still had at home and it was one that James was besotted with as a child, so much so that I had to buy two exactly the same, because if he lost it, there would be hell to pay. Was it coincidence that I had Jimmy and Theresa? No. Was it coincidence that I stayed in their house, something I never do with customers? No. James had brought us both together. What lesson did Theresa get out of my visit and meeting James? She realised she could use her gift to help her in her own work with troubled teenagers, something she is extremely good at.

Music remains our main way of receiving signs from James and a way that I feel he communicates best with me. We could be sitting in a restaurant thinking or talking about him and a certain song will come on with a title that is so apt for James or how we are feeling at the time: 'I'll Stand by You', 'I'll be There', 'Right Here Waiting for You'. I could go on and on but each one comes on at the right time to lift my spirits. Lisa once told me that footprints in the sand would be something I would remember and would cause me to smile. We were going on holiday so I took it that I'd be sitting on the beach and would notice footprints in the sand. But nothing appeared. I took delivery of a new car in July 2009. It had a stereo where the name of each song came up. As I pulled out of the garage to drive home, 'Footprints in the Sand' was playing, by Leona Lewis. Louise and I smiled, knowing this was James' way of telling me he approved.

I will always continue to look for signs. Sometimes they appear more often, whilst other times I can go months without anything but I know it's because I don't need a sign: I know James is there. But getting a sign gives me a boost and is an added bonus.

I know James will be waiting to greet me as I pass over and that's why I am not frightened of dying as I will see him once more. They say heaven is like paradise… but let's hope James hasn't found the shopping malls. I can laugh about this now as I accept he is not here and I have altered my life to deal with it as best I can. I think I am doing pretty well. I decided long ago that I could wallow in my grief or I could pick myself up and make something more of my life, of my business and of my relationships with people, to make James proud, and I will continue to do this until I am no longer here.

I miss James every waking moment but I have surrounded myself with people who love and care for me. If I get down, they pick me up. I don't want people around me who will bring me down. I cannot be a sponge for other peoples' problems or grief as I have a daily struggle to cope with my own. I know James is continually there helping me through the hours. We are still a team but not in the usual way. If James needs to tell me something when I am down, then Lisa calls me out of the blue. She is like my telephone line to my son. OK, it may not be broadband but it's just as good!

Am I bothered that some people think this is weird? No! I get through my day as best I can and I have come a long way since 2005 when I could not even envisage going out, let alone travelling around the world. I still do it all for James, even though he is not here for me to leave anything to. My pride in James is my legacy to him.

LIGHT AT THE END OF A VERY LONG TUNNEL

After the emotions of the court case and sentencing had calmed down, I decided to give into Louise's ten-year pleading and get the dog she always wanted. She had always wanted a cocker spaniel, an orange roan called Scoobi. No other dog – it had to be exactly as she wanted! Lisa had also phoned around this time saying James was telling me to get a puppy so the whole thing now felt right. I made it clear that if we got a dog, Louise was to be responsible for walking him and feeding him. We bought a dog bed, as you do when you have decided to get a dog, and then set about finding him. We printed off the list of breeders from the Kennel Club and Louise phoned some of them. Some had orange roans but were situated some hours' drive away and she did not feel it was right to have a puppy in the car for hours on end. We searched and searched but just could not find a puppy.

One day sitting in the house on my own I decided to take the list and make the calls. I started at the top, went to the middle, then started at the bottom and ended in the middle again – nothing. I then decided to phone the last breeder on the list based in Ascot, Berkshire. A lady answered by the name of Jan. I explained what I wanted and she started to grill me. Had I owned spaniels before? (We both had.) What would happen to a puppy whilst we were at work? I explained the puppy would come to work with us. Jan asked if we had children in the house and I briefly explained what had happened to us. She then told me she had one male puppy left and it was an orange roan. However, she'd had two families come to see him and he just shook with nerves when they picked him up. For this reason Jan had refused to let him go. I arranged to go up there immediately, with Louise, to see it; however, Jan explained that if the dog was nervous with us we could not have him. She was a very caring breeder who wanted her dogs to have a good home.

We arrived at Jan's house just after lunch and she showed us to the puppy. He was gorgeous: so tiny he could almost fit in your hand. Louise picked him up and he started licking her face. We knew straightaway that this was Scoobi and he seemed to know straightaway that he had just met his new Mummy and Daddy! Jan agreed that he had taken to us and agreed to let us have him. We were elated. We arranged to collect him in three weeks' time. It was a very long three weeks, but I somehow knew we were meant to find him, as if James had guided our path.

As soon as Scoobi arrived home with us we fell in love with him. He was the most loving dog anyone could meet. He'd fall asleep on my shoulders; he'd follow us around everywhere; he came into work with us and just lay by our desks. He was everything we wanted and more. Gone were the instructions for Louise to walk him and feed him: we shared the responsibility. We couldn't take our eyes off him. We started off insisting he stay in the kitchen as he was a puppy and all puppies have accidents. From the day he arrived home, we never heard a whimper out of him at night. In fact, some mornings we had to wake him! Again, I felt that James was taking care of Scoobi. They say dogs have a sixth sense and this gave me comfort knowing that Scoobi was probably being watched over by his guardian angel at night.

Sleeping in the kitchen lasted for at least six months and then he made his way upstairs onto our bed. We always said we would not give him treats, until those brown eyes gave us that longing look at mealtimes and we just had to give him a little something. We could not get enough of him. If he was out of our sight for 30 minutes, even though we knew he was asleep upstairs, we had to go and check on him. We were besotted, hook, line and sinker!

Scoobi took over our lives but in the nicest possible way. He came everywhere with us and even followed us into the bathroom when it

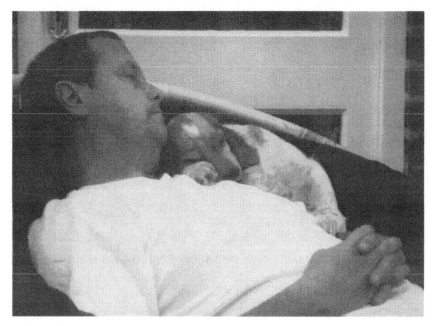

Scoobi asleep on my shoulder

was ablution time! He quickly got into a routine. Scoobi knew when it was treat time so he'd have his evening treat and then take himself off to bed, our bed, where he'd pull back the duvet and tuck himself in.

Of course, not everything went smoothly. At first Scoobi was convinced he was Alan Titchmarsh – he would dig and dig and dig our precious garden. Since James' passing we had busied ourselves in the garden and, pre-Scoobi, it had never looked so good. Post-Scoobi arriving, it looked like a war zone: the lines in my lawn had disappeared and turned into massive pot holes that resembled bunkers! Our hedges had flattened as Scoobi had decided these were now his new outdoor beds so flopped himself in them, making them as flat as the lawn. Gardening became a nightmare as every ten minutes Scoobi leapt up, insisting we cuddle him, so our white gardening clothes frequently had paw prints on them, but we simply didn't care.

Scoobi was the best tonic we needed and I felt like James had found him for us. If Scoobi was human, his character would have been just like James'. Scoobi had to be in the middle of everything. If there was a gang, he had to be in it. He was so playful. He had that look that, even if he had burned down the house, he would probably have gotten away with it. He was so loving – if you asked him for a kiss, he came over and gave you one. He'd wake us up in the morning with a kiss then continually bark as if he was talking to us.

Scoobi loved his toys and had a new one nearly every week. He had a dog bed in nearly every room as well as one at work. He'd sit in the car looking out as if he were being chauffeur-driven. The looks we got from other drivers, I swear they thought he was a statue. If anyone looked at Scoobi, he'd turn his nose in the air and look away – he was a total snob when he wanted to be. He would come into work but at first he refused to walk down the metal stairs that led out from Louise's office so we carried him down, probably ten times a day. Like any dog, he knew he could walk down them but why walk when you can be carried? The postman would put the post through the letterbox and Scoobi would go mad. Anyone who came to the door at work had Scoobi to deal with... well, from the luxury of his bed under the stairs. He is not brave enough to actually confront someone! Scoobi was now the main part of the family, our main focus, and we loved him more than ever.

Taking Scoobi for walks meant we got to know more and more people within our village – not that we knew their names, but simply that they were Woof's Dad or Wag's Mum!! Acknowledging more and more people whilst out walking really hit home how lucky we were to live in a village and able to be comforted by village life. Small communities are one of the best tonics when you have lost someone so dear. Of course, word gets around about what has happened to you but a smaller community knows when to say something and when not to, and neighbours and friends in the village allowed us to grieve as we wanted to grieve and not to grieve how they thought we should be grieving.

After having Scoobi for a number of months, I realised how much I had moved on. James was never forgotten and was constantly on my mind but I could go about my day-to-day life without being consumed with grief. I was always told that the pain of grief would get better as time goes on, and that one day I would wake up and James would not be the only thing on my mind and that is true. I wake up, turn over and look at James' photo and now I can smile when I look at it, knowing that he would be saying to me, "Get up and make the most of your day, Dad." The last thing James would want was me sitting around moping. I had done that in the beginning but I knew I would never feel any better if I carried on in this way, knowing that James would have been angry with me.

The cloud has lifted from above me and I feel that light is now shining through. I do not feel guilty about going away, pleasure or business, as I know that James is always there with me, like my guardian angel. I can talk about him with laughter, without feeling guilty that he is not present in body next to me. If I see people of James' age, I like to hear that they are living life to the full as life is too short. So what if they've had a few too many drinks? So what if they arrived home too late? It's all pointless on the wider scale of life.

I go into work now, hungry for a sale, wanting to build the business up, knowing that James would have come into the business and worked with me. At one point I could not have cared if the business had even continued, let alone make a profit or take on extra customers – but now I am proud of what we have all achieved with the company and I want it to grow and grow.

One of the most important issues that seems to crop up continually is, "Do you have children?" Such a question arises on paper or when speaking to people. Even when I fill in membership applications or to join a committee, the question is always there. Yes, is the answer, and I place an asterisk by the answer and write a small line, "Died, aged 16, in December 2005." When it then comes to an interview, I believe it is important that the panel be made aware that I have experience in bringing up children.

In my travels around the world, setting up new customers for our products, the topic of children always crops up in conversation over dinner or at the bar. I have decided that, as and when this occurs, the answer will always be yes. However, I follow my reply with words such as… "Unfortunately, my son James died in a car accident several years ago, at the age of 16." Most people are shocked and horrified, to say the least, and feel that they should change the subject immediately – always assuming that I do not want to talk about it. I stop them from doing that and I talk freely about James, the life that we had, and how I coped with losing him. I explain how James' death changed me as a person. I love to talk to people about him, even people I have only met on a handful of occasions.

When I know other people have children, I always feel that their inner thoughts are, 'Oh my God, what if that happened to me? I would never cope.' After talking to them, I always say that everyone thinks they will not cope, but somehow people do. You find the strength from somewhere to deal with things, and you have to keep going on the path that has been set out for you. Some people start to ask about what I believe in, and only then do I explain that with all the books I have read, it's my belief that I will see James once more in another world. This is the belief that helps me to live my life day by day.

If you have lost a child, I think you should never ignore the question, "Do you have children?" You do have children and in your own mind you have to try to accept that they are still with you in spirit. I think this is important to remember.

Two years after James passed, I decided to host a dinner for his 18th birthday. I hired a private room at a restaurant in London for family and a select group of friends, all of whom had played a part in James' short life. Years ago I had been given a special bottle of famous Scottish whisky as a wonderful gift from a supplier I was using at the time. It was an extra-old reserve and had been bottled on the day James was born. The inscription on the label read: 'The whisky in this bottle was distilled at the Knockando Distillery and drawn on

9th January 1989. It was drawn from cask and specially bottled to commemorate the birth of James Joseph Bollom.'

It was always my intention to give James this bottle on his 18th birthday, so I decided we would all have a glass and raise a toast for James. We had a wonderful evening. All the men wore black ties and the ladies wore cocktail dresses, and I asked everyone to wear something pink as James loved the colour. Some wore pink cufflinks, dresses, bracelets, socks – everyone really made the effort. I had a pianist there and everyone ended up singing around the piano at the end of the evening – a great tribute to our wonderful boy. The bottle and its case will always serve as a reminder of this special occasion.

A short while ago one of my best friend's ex phoned to say she was moving with her family to Bearsted and could they pop round for a coffee for us to meet her husband and to catch up on old times. Tom, her son, came with her. He was 12 and reminded me so much of James at that age. Like James, he was a boy who was very comfortable in adult company and carried himself so well. Tom said he had taken up golf and that he was hoping to get some new clubs for his forthcoming birthday. I immediately thought of James' full set just sitting there in our study gathering dust. I knew that one day I would have to get rid of them but could not bring myself to. Now the time felt right. I took Tom into the study and asked him to hold a club just to see if they were the right height. They were and I asked him if he'd like them. Tom's face said it all. He was overwhelmed and those few seconds made it all worthwhile. His mum had tears in her eyes, knowing how precious James' things were to me but I knew that they were going to a good home.

I am pleased to say Tom has since joined the local club and I look forward to playing him one day. A while after, Tom's mum, Kate, told me about a dream she had the night I gave Tom the clubs. In the dream all of us were there, and James. James said nothing but simply stood there and smiled. I knew that was his seal of approval.

I will slowly start to give James' possessions away when I feel the time is right. It's not something I urgently need to do but, like anything, one day I will probably wake up and hear someone telling me in my head that now is the time.

I have described many signs in this book; most of them were not looked for. I am told that the more you look for signs, the less you see them. Signs can come when you most need them, but you only get signs if you are open to receiving them. If you cannot learn to live, once a loved one has passed, then I do not believe your loved one can help you in your grief by giving you signs. How will your loved one know when you need a sign if you are clouded in a black fog of grief?

I have told of many signs given to me by James. He continues to show me that he is watching over me. When Louise and I go away, we generally have at least one sign that James is with us, mainly through music by receiving feathers.

The natural need to be surrounded by friends and loved ones, demonstrates the desire to get away for a while from the enormity of consuming grief. At first there is guilt about going away and enjoying yourself, but it is absolutely correct that a change of scenery does help put a different perspective on the grieving process. Getting away from home forces you to go out of the room, to speak to new people, all of whom have no idea of what you have been through. Everyone has their own individual problems or worries, and spending time with others does lift the cloud surrounding you for a while, and allows daylight to sneak through.

Louise and I have often found feathers in our path whilst out walking, or even at home – just a single, white feather. We have a jarful at home of every feather we have been fortunate enough to find and all are pure white. Recently, we were walking along and one fell out of a clear blue sky. There was nothing around us, no trees for birds to sit in, just pure open blue sky. A white feather landed in front of us whilst walking. Where did it come from? I asked. "James," replied Lou, "from heaven." From music being turned down and lights flickering without blowing, it all means something.

I eventually decided to take a look at James' computer login, as we all shared the same computer. I knew his login so typed away. Up came some information, as well as photos, which made me well up; but then I saw the files he had downloaded from his phone. They were short video clips. I watched a couple, and on clicking the third one, the computer froze. The system had to be rebooted to see what went wrong. After rebooting the computer, all was well again. I decided to look at some other files. Bang! It crashed again. I asked Louise to take a look, and she said that she felt that these items were private and that James was trying to tell me he was not ready for me to see them. Maybe I was not strong enough to look at what James had got up to. All other files of the same size opened as usual; it was just James' videos we could not open. I felt it was best left alone and so decided to listen to music that he had on his iTunes. Knowing the most played, I listened to these first.

Some months later, when the computer needed changing, I decided that I was ready to have a look at the phone files I had previously been unable to open. Of course, they opened straightaway, and I could see why James may have thought I was not ready to see them as they showed him talking as well larking about, as usual, with his friends.

I could cope now and I can only assume James knew it was time for me to see them. It showed me how much stronger I had become, and I was now able to face hearing his voice.

At home by my bed there is always a photo of James, so it's the last thing I look at each night and the first thing I see when I wake up. When I travel, this photograph comes with me so my routine never changes.

The only thing I still am unable to do is drive along the road where the crash happened – even four years on, the thought of it fills me with dread. A plaque still remains on the wall and flowers are laid on every anniversary, but I will never visit that site again.

I look on life differently now. I am not afraid of dying; I am afraid of the method of dying but not the actual passing itself as I know

James will be waiting for me. If I did not have this belief, then things might be different, but I have to live my life for me and my beliefs, not what others believe in. Losing someone does make you selfish inasmuch as you do not care what others think any more, but it also makes you selfless when dealing with others. I want to help others more as this gives me pleasure, whether it's simply giving to charity or giving small gifts to loved ones. The smile on their faces means more than it ever did.

The main lesson I have learned from James' passing is that life goes on. Human nature does not dictate that a life should end when you lose someone so dear to you, but you should review your life and make the most of every day. My love for James is stronger than it has ever been. None of us know what is around the corner and life is too short to be upset all day, every day. I know this is not what James would have wanted so I am determined to live my life as I think he would have wanted me to and in a way that he would be proud of.

Until we meet again James

Love you, Dad x

ACKNOWLEDGEMENTS

My thanks go to the nurse who was passing at the time of the accident – without her observations I would never have been able to confirm if James had suffered and I know he did not.

To our Police Family Liaison Officer who put our thoughts and feelings first and was a tower of strength throughout the months after James passed. A truly kind-hearted and gallant gentleman, in every sense of the word.

To the police investigation team who supported us throughout the trial and whose thorough investigation helped us piece together all of the evidence, allowing us to know exactly what had happened on that fateful day. The judge said they had done a first class investigation and we could not agree more.

To James' friends who continue to keep in touch every anniversary, meeting up to celebrate James' life. Hearing your many stories always brings a smile to my face and lifts my spirits. I respect you leaving flowers on James' grave at special times, and when you visit as I know you will never forget him – Lewi, Platt, Jonny, Dave C, Moggie, Jack H, Mills, Fred, Turner, Jack P, Adam S, Miller, Phil E, Littlen, Cara, Lauren and Hannah, to name a few – too many to mention them all.

To Vicki – I know James will always have a special place in your heart. Thank you for setting up his Facebook remembrance page – I often read all of the tributes on there.

To my loyal friends – who could ask for better? Nic & Rob, John, Kathy & Mark, Mark & Claire, Paul & Pauline, Sally & Reg, John &

Collette, Tracey, Ann & George. You all helped me so much during that fateful week, taking a huge worry off my shoulders – and you continue to help me to this day.

My thanks to Mark Brown for being a friend to James amongst other things.

To Lisa Jayne who, as you have read in this book, has given me so much help and understanding due to this terrible tragedy and who continues to do so. Thank you from the bottom of my heart for showing me the way forward and, more importantly, communicating with James.

To my wife's parents, Beryl and Neil, who treated James as if he was one of their own grandsons, and for the love and support they have given to us.

To my family, who have experienced a loss that no family should have to suffer. You have helped me come though this terrible tragedy and we have become much stronger as a family unit which I treasure.

And finally my wife – without her by my side throughout this terrible time I would have suffered many a setback in my grieving process. She continues to be a tower of strength to me and I thank her for her support in writing this book.

* * * * *